Anonymus

Intermediate Education Board for Ireland report 1897

Anonymus

Intermediate Education Board for Ireland report 1897

ISBN/EAN: 9783742810212

Manufactured in Europe, USA, Canada, Australia, Japa

Cover: Foto ©ninafisch / pixelio.de

Manufactured and distributed by brebook publishing software
(www.brebook.com)

Anonymus

Intermediate Education Board for Ireland report 1897

REPORT

INTERMEDIATE EDUCATION BOARD

FOR IRELAND

FOR THE YEAR 1897.

Presented to Parliament by Command of Her Majesty.

DUBLIN:
PRINTED FOR HER MAJESTY'S STATIONERY OFFICE,
By ALEXANDER THOM & CO. (Limited), ABBEY-STREET.

And to be purchased, either directly or through any Bookseller, from
HODGES, FIGGIS, & CO., (Limited), 104, Grafton-street, Dublin; or
EYRE & SPOTTISWOODE, East Harding-street, Fleet-street, E.C.; or
JOHN MENZIES & CO., 12, Hanover-street, Edinburgh, and
90, West Nile-street, Glasgow.

1898.

C—8798.] *Price 7d.*

CONTENTS.

REPORT

INTERMEDIATE EDUCATION BOARD

FOR IRELAND

FOR THE YEAR 1897.

TO HIS EXCELLENCY, GEORGE HENRY,
EARL CADOGAN, K.G.,

LORD LIEUTENANT GENERAL AND GENERAL GOVERNOR OF IRELAND.

MAY IT PLEASE YOUR EXCELLENCY,

We, the Commissioners of Intermediate Education (Ireland), submit to your Excellency this our Nineteenth Report.

The number of students who gave notice of their intention to present for examination in 1897 was:—

Boys.	Girls.	Total.
7,149	2,173	9,005

being an increase of 142, or 2·0 per cent., in the case of boys and an increase of 89, or 1·6 per cent., in the case of girls; and a total increase of 1·9 per cent. on the corresponding numbers in 1896; and a total increase of 0·5 per cent. on the corresponding numbers in 1895.

In the last ten years the numbers were respectively as follows :—

Year.	Boys.	Girls.	Total.
1888	4,905	1,524	6,529
1889	5,261	1,878	7,139
1890	4,341	1,428	5,769
1891	4,103	1,444	5,687
1892	4,114	1,672	6,336
1893	5,720	1,866	7,586
1894	4,979	2,067	8,046
1895	6,765	2,253	9,018
1896	7,040	2,384	9,124
1897	7,181	2,422	9,603

See Table L.

The number of students who presented themselves for examination in 1897 was:—

Boys.	Girls.	Total.
6,661	2,216	8,877

being an increase of 158 or 2·4 per cent. in the case of boys, and an increase of 8 or 0·4 per cent. in the case of girls, and a total increase of 160 or 1·9 per cent. on the corresponding numbers in 1896.

In the last ten years the numbers were respectively as follows :—

Year.	Boys.	Girls.	Total.
1888, . .	4,531	1,507	6,038
1889, . .	4,838	1,895	6,533
1890, . .	4,948	1,228	6,226
1891, . .	4,866	1,300	6,166
1892, . .	4,294	1,465	5,759
1893, . .	5,365	1,709	7,074
1894, . .	5,314	1,558	7,802
1895, . .	6,267	2,056	8,323
1896, . .	6,505	2,206	8,711
1897, . .	6,661	2,216	8,877

See Appendix V.

The examinations for 1897, which commenced on 14th June and extended over twelve days, were held at 268 centres, in 90 different localities.

The following Table shows the distribution of Centres between the Four Provinces :—

Centres.	Leinster.	Ulster.	Munster.	Connaught.	Totals.
Centres for Boys. .	77	41	60	14	192
Centres for Girls. ,	27	28	13	3	71
Total, . .	104	69	73	17	263

One hundred and ninety-three gentlemen and seventy-two ladies were employed as Centre Superintendents, being an average of one Superintendent to every 34 boys and to every 31 girls examined, respectively.

The number of students who passed the Examinations in 1897 was :— See Table III.

Boys.	Girls.	Total.
1,184	1404	5,538

In the last ten years the numbers were respectively as follows :—

Year.	Boys.	Girls.	Total.
1848,	2,572	1,223	4,064
1849,	2,844	1,171	4,016
1890,	2,333	767	3,100
1891,	3,304	771	4,078
1892,	2,839	781	3,628
1893,	3,042	933	4,990
1894,	3,419	1,104	4,623
1895,	3,783	1,190	4,973
1896,	3,763	1,213	4,968
1897,	4,134	1,404	5,538

The proportion per cent. of those examined who passed in 1897 was :—

Boys.	Girls.	Boys and Girls.
62·1	63·6	63·4

The proportions in the last ten years were respectively as follows :—

Year.	Boys.	Girls.	Boys and Girls.
1888,	62·1	51·1	67·5
1889,	58·7	60·2	61·3
1890,	60·1	58·3	59·2
1891,	30·7	59·5	59·6
1892,	50·1	53·6	51·7
1893,	57·7	55·0	57·3
1894,	58·6	50·2	58·0
1895,	60·4	57·9	59·8
1896,	57·7	51·9	57·
1897,	62·1	63·6	62·1

Exclusive of over-age students the proportion *per cent* of those examined who passed was :—

Boys.	Girls.	Boys and Girls.
64·6	63·5	63·6

Exclusive of over-age students the proportions in the last eight years were as follows:—

Year.	Boys.	Girls.	Boys and Girls.
1890,	38·0	30·4	39·1
1891,	50·7	59·0	39·3
1892,	50·4	55·5	51·8
1893,	30·6	57·2	50·
1894,	60·3	50·9	60·2
1895,	61·2	60·3	61·5
1896,	56·9	54·7	56·1
1897,	63·8	63·8	63·8

The number of students to whom were awarded £50 Prizes (Senior Grade), and Exhibitions in the Middle, Junior, and Preparatory Grades was :—

Boys, 388 ; Girls, 134 ; Total, 522.

The number of students to whom were awarded prizes in books was :—

Boys, 402 ; Girls, 152 ; Total, 554.

The number of students to whom were awarded Prizes for Composition under Rule 52 was :— *See Table VII.*

Boys, 113 ; Girls, 52 ; Total, 165.

The number of students to whom were awarded Commercial Prizes under Rule 49 was:— *See Table VIII.*

Boys, 29 ; Girls, 0 ; Total, 29.

Three large Gold Medals were awarded to Boys, and three to Girls, for First Places in the several Grades. Eleven Gold Medals were awarded to Boys, and six to Girls, for excellence in Special Subjects. *See Table IX.*

The number of students to whom were awarded Special Money Prizes in lieu of Medals under Rule 49 was :—

Boys, 1 ; Girls, 2 ; Total, 3.

The amount of Results Fees paid to Managers of Schools on account of the Examinations in 1897 was :— *See Appendix IV.*

Boys, £30,615 12s. 5d. ; Girls, £12,254 18s. 1d. ;
Total, £44,870 10s. 0d.

Of the students, 5,538, who passed the Examination, Results Fees were paid on 5,240, being an average Fee of £9 6s. 6d. per student.

The following Table shows the distribution of Results Fees between the Four Provinces, and the number of Schools in each Province, to the Managers of which Results Fees were paid :—

PROVINCES.	Amount of Results Fees paid.			No. of Schools.		
	Boys.	Girls.	TOTAL.	Boys	Girls	Total.
	£ s. d.	£ s. d.	£ s. d.			
Leinster,	14,967 4 6	4,673 6 5	19,643 10 11	75	53	128
Ulster,	7,856 8 0	5,171 7 2	13,027 15 2	53	79	132
Munster,	11,025 11 6	1,903 7 0	13,503 18 6	62	23	85
Connaught,	2,166 8 2	414 17 6	2,581 5 8	29	7	27
Gross Total,	34,615 12 2	12,254 18 1	47,870 10 0	512	153	367

The values of the Burke Memorial Prizes awarded in 1897 were :—

Boys—	Girls —
First Prize, £14 16s. 0d.	Prize, £9 5s. 0d.
Second Prize, £9 5s. 0d.	

FINANCE.

Our Balance Sheet for the year 1897, in respect of the original Endowment (Table X. *infra*), shows a surplus of £1,918 6s. 2d. (including a sum of £943 10s. 6d., Income Tax, to be refunded). Of this amount £1,492 8s. 6d. is the uninvested surplus of 1896, and a sum of £1,575 12s. was realised by sale of portion of the invested surpluses of former years. The net deficit as between Income and Expenditure for 1897 is thus £1,189 12s. 4d., to which may be added liabilities estimated at £250.

The Local Taxation Account (see Table XI.) shows that the Receipts under the Local Taxation (Customs and Excise) Act, and as interest on securities, amounted to £53,182 14s. 6d., and that the Expenditure from that account on Results Fees and Exhibitions for 1897 was £52,037 2s. 2d., the excess of Income over Expenditure being thus £1,145 12s. 4d.

Taking both Accounts into consideration, our total Income from all sources in 1897 has exceeded our Expenditure in that year by £6.

The period for which interest at 3½ per cent. payable by the Land Commission and guaranteed by the Treasury on our original Endowment of £1,000,000 sterling expired in February, 1897, and negotiations with the Land Commission resulted in the renewal of their debt to the Board for ten years, at 2½ per cent. interest, guaranteed by the Treasury. The income from our original Endowment has, consequently, been diminished by the sum of £5,000 per annum.

EDUCATION.

The conditions of passing the Examination generally were identical with those in force in 1896, with the exception that the restriction in Rule 38 of the Rules for 1896* was withdrawn.

* "38. No student presenting himself for examination in the Commercial portion of any of the following Languages—English, French, German, Italian, or Spanish—shall be eligible for examination in Greek."

The per-centages of Students of the prescribed ages examined in the different Grades who Passed were, compared with the percentages in 1800, as follows:—

GRADE	Boys.		Girls.	
	1897.	1898.	1897.	1898.
Preparatory, . .	57	57 1	61 9	55
Junior, . . .	67	67 9	67	67 7
Middle, . . .	55 9	58 3	73	69 1
Senior, . . .	73 1	73 1	72	64 4

Turning to the Commercial side of our Examinations, the number of students who qualified for Commercial Certificates was 105 (103 Boys and 2 Girls). The number of Special Commercial Prizes awarded was 20 (Boys).

A number of other students, as in previous years, who did not aim at obtaining Commercial Certificates, availed themselves of the opportunity of presenting themselves for examination in certain of the Commercial subjects.

Detailed information respecting the answering of students, Boys and Girls, in the different subjects will be found in the Extracts from the Reports of the Examiners (Appendix III.), copies of which were transmitted to all Managers of Schools in Ireland to whom Results Fees were paid in 1897.

TABLE I.—Showing the Number of Students who presented themselves for Examination in the last ten years, respectively.

YEAR.	PREPARATORY GRADE.									
	1888.	1889.	1890.	1891.	1892.	1893.	1894.	1895.	1896.	1897.
Boys . . .	—	—	—	—	1,429	1,313	2,199	2,546	3,075	3,407
Girls. . .	—	—	—	—	391	472	572	418	601	710
Total, . .	—	—	—	—	1,820	2,365	2,681	2,931	3,663	4,141

TABLE L—Showing the Number of Students who presented themselves

	JUNIOR GRADE.									
YEAR,	1890	1888	1890	1891	1892	1893	1894	1895	1896	1897
Boys—of the prescribed age,	2,869	3,375	3,670	3,004	2,177	2,467	2,346	2,456	2,736	2,645
Do., Over-age,	125	181	91	187	—	240	221	25	811	131
Total,	2,714	3,678	3,361	3,171	7,177	2,667	2,721	2,662	2,071	2,179
Girls—of the prescribed age,	1,103	1,277	716	641	744	779	801	929	94	774
Do., Over-age,	12	11	12	12	—	50	21	29	24	84
Total,	1,311	1,511	834	844	744	527	977	1,011	1,031	1,026
Gross Total,	1,379	5,217	4,077	4,196	2,921	3,434	3,689	3,662	4,116	4,249

	SENIOR GRADE.									
YEAR,	1888	1889	1890	1891	1892	1893	1894	1895	1896	1897
Boys—of the prescribed age,	244	274	218	224	114	200	219	230	218	224
Do., Over-age,	7	10	11	4	7	40	47	75	70	68
Total,	231	284	340	270	702	763	242	307	642	307
Girls—of the prescribed age,	104	171	152	96	51	94	80	102	121	143
Do., Over-age,	3	4	1	3	1	4	7	13	16	12
Total,	115	135	152	94	77	77	102	110	149	164
Gross Total,	343	119	343	324	287	343	364	113	439	463

for Examination in the last ten years, respectively—*continued.*

MIDDLE GRADE.

1888.	1889.	1890.	1891.	1892.	1893.	1894.	1895.	1896.	1897.	Year.
6c3	517	434	421	133	509	564	61–	501	464	Boys—of the prescribed age.
171	34	15	94	-	71	130	178	172	144	Do., Over-age.
364	641	549	637	4x3	576	704	676	785	742	Total.
271	146	237	211	277	542	125	641	296	979	Girls—of the prescribed age.
9	17	6	9	-	26	28	46	40	30	Do., Over-age.
280	315	271	530	277	269	167	710	358	634	Total.
842	697	764	701	716	644	971	682	1,121	1,084	Grand Total.

TOTAL.

1888.	1889.	1890.	1891.	1872.	1893.	1891.	1895.	1896.	1897.	Year.
4,402	4,298	3,973	4,721	4,797	4,818	4,372	4,109	4,945	5,111	Boys—of the prescribed age.
149	146	299	135	7	357	644	646	550	547	Do., Over-age.
4,441	4,425	3,943	5,906	4,894	4,295	4,918	4,747	4,099	5,941	Total.
1,884	1,463	1,771	1,276	1,144	1,616	1,744	1,965	2,852	2,970	Girls—of the prescribed age.
84	33	22	21	1	61	117	163	149	199	Do., Over-age.
1,467	1,295	1,293	1,298	1,195	1,705	1,664	2,234	2,709	2,319	Total.
6,935	6,525	6,726	5,164	6,759	6,071	7,659	6,373	6,721	6,557	Grand Total.

TABLE 11. Showing the Days and Hours at which Examinations in the several subjects of the Programme were held in 1867.

Monday, 10th June									
Tuesday, 11th June									
Wednesday, 12th June									
Thursday, 13th June	NO EXAMINATION								
Friday, 14th June									
Saturday, 15th June									

* Girls only.

[continued

TABLE III.—Showing the number of

	PREPARATORY GRADE			JUNIOR GRADE			MIDDLE
—	Ex-amined.	Passed.	Proportion per cent. of Passes.	Ex-amined.	Passed.	Proportion per cent. of Passes.	Ex-amined.
Boys—of the prescribed age,	2,427	1,643	67·7	2,843	1,707	60·	604
Do., Over-age,	-	-		331	165	49·4	144
Total,	2,427	1,643	67·7	3,173	1,873	58·9	748
Girls—of the prescribed age,	714	442	61·9	995	617	63·	220
Do., Over-age,	-	-	-	85	54	58·9	30
Total,	714	442	61·9	1,080	673	61·7	256
Gross Total,	3,141	2,085	68·4	4,253	2,543	59·8	1,004

TABLE IV.—Showing for each subject (1) the number of students who passed failed, and (4) the total number examined; also the proportion and (6) who passed

BOYS.

Preparatory Grade (Of the Prescribed Age).	SUBJECTS.				
	Greek.	Latin.	English.	French.	German.
Passed with Honors,	96	409	871	1,047	23
" without Honors,	45	419	1,219	810	14
Failed,	45	410	320	320	6
Total Examined,	186	1,240	2,420	3,187	43
Proportion per cent. who passed with Honors,	50·8	32·4	36·	45·6	41·9
Ditto, without Honors,	23·4	33·8	41·6	38·0	34·8
Total Per-centage passed,	75·2	66·2	87·6	82·7	86·1
(Over Age).*					
Passed with Honors,					
" without Honors,					
Failed,					
Total Examined,					
Proportion per cent. who passed with Honors,					
Ditto, without Honors,					

* Over Age Students were all

Students who passed the Examination.

Grade.		Senior Grade.				Total.			
Passed.	Proportion per cent. of Passes.	2r. amined.	Passed.	Proportion per cent. of Passes.	Re-amined.	Passed.	Proportion per cent. of Passes.		
341	80·9	225	186	78·1	8,114	4,580	69·3	Boys—of the prescribed age.
54	81·5	89	85	80·7	547	254	46·4	Do., Over-age.
928	80·7	807	231	73·	5,901	4,134	82·1	Total.
105	79·	148	108	73·	2,078	1,837	60·9	Girls—of the prescribed age.
14	46·7	18	7	63·8	188	77	86·9	Do., Over-age.
179	88·9	186	110	70·6	2,316	1,604	83·9	Total.
877	87·6	469	831	71·6	8,877	5,338	82·4	Gross Total.

with Honors, (2) the number who passed without Honors, (3) the number who
per cent. to those examined of those who (5) passed with Honors,
without Honors.

BOYS.

	Subjects.					Preparatory Grade (Of the Prescribed Age).
Italian.	Greek.	Arithmetic.	Euclid.	Algebra.	Drawing.	
43	181	854	820	683	718	Passed with Honors.
23	91	543	646	352	487	without Honors.
16	43	897	725	460	310	Failed.
71	214	3,404	2,943	1,475	1,690	Total Examined.
54·6	84·6	32·9	97·5	47·2	42·	Proportion per cent. who passed with Honors.
89·3	81·9	33·1	81·1	29·2	37·6	Ditto, without Honors.
89·9	83·8	71·	67·6	76·4	88·3	Total Per-centage passed.
						(Over Age).*
						Passed with Honors.
						without Honors.
						Failed.
						Total Examined.
						Proportion per cent. who passed with Honors.
						Ditto, without Honors.

Eighth for Preparatory Grade.

TABLE IV.—Showing for each subject (1) the number of students who passed
failed, and (4) the total number examined; also the proportions
and (6) who passed

BOYS.

Junior Grade (Of the Prescribed Age).	Greek	Latin	English	Commercial English	French	Commercial French	German	Commercial German	Italian	Commercial Italian	Spanish
Passed with Honors, . .	185	603	465	18	1,268	70	54		91		3
„ without Honors, . .	147	638	1,634	150	170	103	37		15		1
Failed, ...	327	580	425	50	541	60	71		3		.
Total Examined, . .	663	1,821	2,524	857	2,753	249	64		73		8
Proportion per cent. who passed with Honors.	232	279	189	193	458	57	607		712		78
Ditto, without Honors.	371	37	587	691	395	379	373		19		5
Total Percentage passed.	813	579	79	673	87	849	778	,	912		187
(Over Age.)											
Passed with Honors, .	10	19	87	1	39	.	1	.	.	.	1
„ without Honors,	21	69	613	15	159	7	.	.	1	.	.
Failed . . .	64	137	72	11	116	9	.	.	.	.	.
Total Examined, . .	91	529	385	27	306	12	1	.	1	.	1
Proportion per cent. who passed with Honors.	119	92	461	37	129	109	.	:	.	.	109
Ditto, without Honors.	29	595	67	573	571	577	.	.	109	.	.
Total Percentage passed.	179	545	791	571	67	671	109	.	109	.	109

with Honors, (2) the number who passed without Honors, (3) the number who
per cent. to those examined of those who (5) passed with Honors,
without Honors—*continued.*

BOYS.

Commercial Speech	Greek	Arithmetic	Book-keeping	Latin	Algebra	Natural Philosophy	Chemistry	Drawing	Shorthand	Junior Grade (Of the Prescribed Age).
.	110	1,289	561	465	622	46	30	51	166	Passed with Honors.
.	91	682	463	1,185	639	126	90	629	193	„ without Honors.
.	41	701	346	1,129	1,448	179	198	411	199	Failed.
.	249	2,622	683	2,775	2,89·	351	318	1,331	658	Total Examined.
.	43·0	47·6	37·6	16·7	23·3	13·7	16·0	27·3	25·7	Proportion per cent. who passed with Honors.
.	35·6	24·7	41·6	47·6	38·9	37·7	38·3	47·6	29·1	Ditto, without Honors.
.	77·1	72·2	79·2	62·7	61·6	57·1	44·3	67·3	67·8	Total Percentage passed.
										(Over Age.)
.	1	139	50	70	23	1	6	30	5	Passed with Honors.
.	6	156	64	363	36	19	7	34	14	„ without Honors.
.	1	17	37	148	155	15	5	37	15	Failed.
.	6	330	92	381	274	35	11	119	44	Total Examined.
.	23	343	25	49	91	39	163	375	140	Proportion per cent. who passed with Honors.
.	87	476	161	197	306	373	85	474	321	Ditto, without Honors.
.	75	701	719	548	507	571	445	649	44	Total Percentage passed.

TABLE IV.—Showing for each subject (1) the number of students who passed
failed, and (4) the total number examined; also the proportion
and (6) who passed

BOYS.

Middle Grade (Of the Prescribed Age.)	SUBJECTS										
	Greek	Latin	English	Commercial English	French	Commercial French	German	Commercial German	Italian	Commercial Italian	Spanish
Passed with Honors . . .											
„ without Honors . .											
Failed											
Total Examined . .											
Proportion per cent. who passed with Honors.											
Ditto, without Honors.											
Total Per-centage passed.											
(Over Age.)											
Passed with Honors, . .											
„ without Honors. .											
Failed, . . .											
Total Examined, . .											
Proportion per cent. who passed with Honors.											
Ditto, without Honors.											

with Honors, (2) the number who passed without Honors, (3) the number who
per cent. to those examined of those who (5) passed with Honors,
without Honors—*continued.*

BOYS.

Commercial Spanish	Celtic	Arithmetic	Book-keeping	Euclid	Algebra	Natural Philosophy	Chemistry	Drawing	Shorthand	French Writing	Middle Grade (Or the Prescribed Age).
	23	25	65	185	183	16	16	13	26	19	Passed with Honors,
	20	183	86	811	176	34	31	46	86	17	„ without Honors.
	8	179	11	87	209	50	7	78	31	2	Failed.
	61	383	138	384	528	117	11	144	36	38	Total Examined.
	870	879	572	517	301	137	311	175	41	86	Proportion per cent. who passed with Honors.
	383	389	181	51.	548	436	481	81.5	89	447	Ditto, without Honors.
	879	886	819	834	681	483	530	858	89	847	Total Per-centage passed.
											(Over Age).
		15	5	21	10		1	2	1	6	Passed with Honors.
		8	40	8	23	8	6	6	8		„ without Honors.
		60	2	28	84	39	4	13	2		Failed.
	3	148	15	140	118	14	8	23	6	6	Total Examined.
		135	273	271	51		34	87	20	80	Proportion per cent. who passed with Honors.
	81	371	133	380	21	280 ; 51.5	201	87		Ditto, without Honors.
	187	507	848	871	394	896	87	473	89	648	Total Per-centage passed.

TABLE IV.—Showing for each subject (1) the number of students who passed failed, and (4) the total number examined; also the proportion and (6) who passed

BOYS.

Senior Grade (Of the Prescribed Age).	Greek	Latin	English	Commercial English	French	Commercial French	German	Commercial German	Italian	Commercial Italian	Spanish
Passed with Honors, . . .					10	19	23		13		
„ without Honors, . .					46		19		3		
Failed, ...	17		23			3	3				
Total Examined, . .		110				20	36		17		
Proportion per cent. who passed with Honors,											
Ditto, without Honors,											
Total Percentage passed,											
(Over Age.)											
Passed with Honors, . .	7		6		17	1					
„ without Honors, . .					44						
Failed, ...	16		16								
Total Examined, . .		61									
Proportion per cent. who passed with Honors											
Ditto, without Honors,											

with Honors, (2) the number who passed without Honors, (3) the number who
per cent. to those examined of those who (5) passed with Honors,
without Honors—*continued.*

BOYS.

					Subjects					Senior Grade (or the Prescribed Age).
Commercial Spanish.	Celtic.	Algebra and Arithmetic.	Euclid.	Plane Trigonometry.	Natural Philosophy.	Chemistry.	Drawing.	Shorthand.	Plain Writing.	
.	16	64	65	44	18	1	7	3	13	Passed with Honors.
.	8	76	130	5	30	5	6	10	5	„ without Honors.
.	.	74	16	30	19	6	1	3	.	Failed.
.	30	220	228	181	54	14	15	15	21	Total Examined.
.	70	148	25	309	224	17	107	27	77·1	Proportion per cent. who passed with Honors.
.	37	379	415	32	449	347	8·73	457	24·6	Ditto, without Honors.
.	107	576	853	533	572	448	87	637	100	Total Percentage passed.
										(Over Age).
.	.	6	16	7	.	.	.	.	8	Passed with Honors.
.	8	14	68	7	1	1	1	.	3	„ without Honors.
.	.	13	36	16	6	.	.	.	.	Failed.
.	1	61	60	38	7	1	1	.	8	Total Examined.
.	.	76	146	81·9	.	.	.	.	97	Proportion per cent. who passed with Honors.
.	100	374	71·	719	378	100	100	.	8	Ditto, without Honors.
.	100	632	853	576	378	107	167	.	106	Total Percentage passed.

TABLE IV.—Showing for each subject (1) the number of students who passed
failed, and (4) the total number examined; also the proportion
and (6) who passed

BOYS.

Total in all Grades (Of the Prescribed Age).	SUBJECTS.											
	Greek	Latin	English	Commercial English	French	Commercial French	German	Commercial German	Italian	Commercial Italian	Spanish	Commercial Spanish
Passed with Honors . .	418	1,161	1,513	19	2,340	101	143	17	146	9	3	
„ without Honors .	388	1,116	2,376	163	1,742	No	61	8	13		1	
Failed	871	1,573	1,373	116	820	68	31		14			
Total Examined . . .	1,865	4,828	6,089	369	6,591	355	327	14	280	9	4	
Proportion per cent. who passed with Honors.	22·5	293	247	5·1	35·8	387	679	687	712	100	75·	
Ditto, without Honors .	17·4	513	441	535	30·5	458	207	142	31·9		29·	
Total Percentage passed .	41·9	534	587	63·3	79·5	513	716	107	531	147	107	
(Over Age.)												
Passed with Honors . .	51	33	46	8	130	1	1				1	
„ without Honors . .	67	110	329	68	365	13			3			
Failed	60	350	159	11	370	12	1					
Total Examined . . .	159	350	543	95	594	33	2		1		1	
Proportion per cent. who passed with Honors.	117	7·6	153	47	25·0	31	46·				100	
Ditto, without Honors .	37·3	34·	43·1	53·1	107	37·6			100			
Total Percentage passed .	49·0	41·3	707	60·3	66·3	50·6	50·		10·0		100	

with Honors, (2) the number who passed without Honors, (3) the number who
per cent. to those examined of those who (3) passed with Honors,
without Honors—*continued.*

BOYS.

												Total in all Grades of the Prescribed Age.
	Arithmetic	Book-keeping	Euclid	Algebra	Algebra and Arithmetic	Plane Trigonometry	Natural Philosophy	Chemistry	Drawing	Shorthand	Free Writing	
Oral												
508	1,236	220	1,836	1,818	64	64	78	60	1,818	148	34	Passed with Honors.
180	1,964	618	2,388	1,835	73	58	312	118	1,777	225	13	„ without Honors.
184	1,877	267	1,807	1,808	74	48	258	132	1,913	329	8	Failed.
872	5,810	1,180	4,778	4,701	206	181	638	280	6,368	688	66	Total Examined.
												Proportion per cent. who passed with Honors.
												Ditto, without Honors.
												Total Percentage passed.
												(Over Age.)
1	123	20	64	28	8	7	1	3	30	8	7	Passed with Honors.
2	148	48	240	109	14	1	18	11	64	61	2	„ without Honors.
1	140	28	184	249	53	18	37	9	48	84	.	Failed.
8	471	111	578	888	81	37	68	23	143	8	9	Total Examined.
												Proportion per cent. who passed with Honors.
												Ditto, without Honors.
												Total Percentage passed.

Table IV.—Showing for each subject (1) the number of students who passed
failed, and (4) the total number examined; also the proportion
and (0) who passed

GIRLS.

Preparatory Grade (Of the Prescribed Age).	Subjects.					
	Greek.	Latin.	English.	French.	German.	Italian
Passed with Honors, ...	.	32	273	230	81	11
„ without Honors, ...	.	66	263	267	41	15
Failed, ...	2	89	71	154	27	11
Total Examined, . .	2	187	712	711	155	37
Proportion per cent. who passed with Honors,	.	17·1	39·2	35·2	35·2	29·7
Ditto, without Honors, . . .	.	35·2	36·6	37·3	39·1	40·5
Total Percentage passed . .	.	52·1	99·	72·7	62·3	78·5
(Over Age).*						
Passed with Honors, ...						
„ without Honors,						
Failed, ...						
Total Examined, . . .						
Proportion per cent. who passed with Honors,						
Ditto, without Honors, . . .						

* Over Age Students were not

with Honors, (2) the number who passed without Honors, (3) the number who
per cent. to those examined of those who (5) passed with Honors,
without Honors—*continued.*

GIRLS

	Grades.				Preparatory Grade (for the Prescribed Age).
Gelic.	Arith-metic.	Eucild	Algebra.	Drawing.	
1	151	57	183	321	Passed with Honors.
3	213	83	147	294	„ without Honors.
.	397	118	67	23	Failed.
4	763	258	449	638	Total Examined.
25·	21·5	21·1	47·7	50·3	Proportion per cent. who passed with Honors.
73·	16·3	32·2	35·9	46·3	Ditto, without Honors.
103·	57·8	51·3	83·6	96·5	Total Percentage passed.
					(Over Age.)
					Passed with Honors.
					„ without Honors.
					Failed.
					Total Examined.
					Proportion per cent. who passed with Honors.
					Ditto, without Honors

* Eligible for Preparatory Grade.

Table IV.—Showing for each subject (1) the number of students who passed
failed, and (4) the total number examined; also the proportion
and (5) who passed

GIRLS.

Junior Grade (Of the Prescribed Age)	SUBJECTS										
	Greek	Latin	English	Commercial English	French	Commercial French	German	Commercial German	Italian	Commercial Italian	Spanish	Commercial Spanish
Passed with Honors												
„ without Honors												
Failed												
Total Examined												
Proportion per cent. who passed with Honors												
Ditto, without Honors												
Total Percentage passed												
(Over Age.)												
Passed with Honors												
„ without Honors												
Failed												
Total Examined												
Proportion per cent. who passed with Honors												
Ditto, without Honors												
Total Percentage passed												

with Honors, (2) the number who passed without Honors, (3) the number who
per cent. to those examined of those who (5) passed with Honors,
without Honors—*continued.*

GIRLS.

												Junior Grade (Of the Prescribed Age).
Celtic.	Arithmetic.	Book-keeping.	Euclid.	Algebra.	Natural Philosophy.	Chemistry.	Botany.	Drawing.	Music.	Domestic Economy.	Shorthand.	
7	983	47	38	115	.	1	18	183	116	155	13	Passed with Honors.
6	957	58	143	188	5	2	43	263	267	304	13	„ without Honors.
.	962	19	185	273	.	.	19	294	239	228	17	Failed.
13	959	115	366	573	5	3	81	714	399	764	43	Total Examined.
79	357	353	72	196	.	333	374	359	191	374	354	Proportion per cent. who passed with Honors.
30	416	637	472	371	157	687	571	443	413	513	379	Ditto. without Honors.

Table IV.—Showing for each subject (1) the number of students who passed
failed, and (4) the total number examined; also the proportion
and (6) who passed

GIRLS.

Middle Grade (Of the Prescribed Age).	Subjects.											
	Greek	Latin	English	Commercial English	French	Commercial French	German	Commercial German	Italian	Commercial Italian	Spanish	Commercial Spanish
Passed with Honors,	9	87	17	3	173	5	86	2	27	1	.	.
without Honors.	7	44	160	8	68	11	19	9	1	.	.	.
Failed.	.	27	90	7	6	19	7	.	1	.	.	.
Total Examined.	19	86	280	23	273	33	91	8	24	1	.	.

with Honors, (2) the number who passed without Honors, (3) the number who
per cent. to those examined of those who (3) passed with Honors,
without Honors—*continued.*

GIRLS.

Subjects.													Middle Grade (Of the Prescribed Age).
Celtic.	Arithmetic.	Book-keeping.	Euclid.	Algebra.	Natural Philosophy.	Chemistry.	Botany.	Drawing.	Music.	Domestic Economy.	Shorthand.	Freak Writing.	
													Passed with Honors.
													„ without Honors.
													Failed.
													Total Examined.
													Proportion per cent. who passed with Honors.
													Ditto without Honors.
													Total Percentage passed.
													(Over Age).
													Passed with Honors.
													„ without Honors.
													Failed.
													Total Examined.
													Proportion per cent. who passed with Honors.
													Ditto without Honors.
													Total Per-centage passed.

TABLE IV.—Showing for each subject (1) the number of students who passed
failed, and (4) the total number examined; also the proportion
and (0) who passed

GIRLS.

Senior Grade (Of the Prescribed Age).	SUBJECTS.											
	Greek.	Latin.	English.	Commercial English.	French.	Commercial French.	German.	Commercial German.	Italian.	Commercial Italian.	Spanish.	Commercial Spanish.
Passed with Honors,	5	11	21	4	20	8	43	4	17	2	7	8
„ without Honors.	7	21	80	7	15	18	77	6	1	1	.	.
Failed.	.	16	23	2	12	4	8	1	1	.	.	.
Total Examined,	5	65	123	16	143	54	78	7	19	8	7	2
Proportion per cent. who passed with Honors.	71·4	21·2	18·8	27·8	0	37·3	42·1	52·0	25·5	64·7	100	100
Ditto, without Honors.	57·1	47·7	57·9	50	53·4	67	54·4	67·1	52	37·3	.	.
Total Per-centage passed.	100	67·1	78·7	72·6	80·6	67·3	96·7	67·7	81·1	100	100	100
(Over Age).												
Passed with Honors,	.	.	.	.	8	.	1	.	.	.	.	.
„ without Honors,	1	1	0	1	10	2	4	.	.	.	.	.
Failed.	.	.	4	.	1	1	2	.	.	.	.	.
Total Examined,	1	1	13	1	60	3	7	.	.	.	.	.
Proportion per cent. who passed with Honors.	.	.	.	.	13·4	.	14·3	.	.	.	.	.
Ditto, without Honors.	100	100	67·2	100	78·0	67	57·1	.	.	.	.	.
Total Per-centage passed,	100	100	67·7	100	80·6	67	71·4	.	.	.	.	.

with Honors, (3) the number who passed without Honors, (3) the number who
per cent. to those examined of them who (5) passed with Honors,
without Honors—*continued.*

GIRLS.

	SUBJECTS.											Senior Grade (Of the Prescribed Age).
Celtic.	Arithmetic and Arithmetic.	Euclid.	Plane Trigonometry.	Natural Philosophy.	Chemistry.	Botany.	Drawing.	Music.	Domestic Economy.	Shorthand.	French Writing.	
.	18	17	9	.	.	4	20	13	12	.	3	Passed with Honors.
.	10	53	11	6	1	3	14	43	14	1	.	,, without Honors.
.	23	14	13	.	1	.	18	14	9	1	.	Failed.
.	41	64	53	6	4	5	61	68	120	2	3	Total Examined.
.	176	276	67	.	.	60	576	211	171	.	100	Proportion per cent. who passed with Honors.
.	371	47	324	100	67	60	374	611	341	50	.	Ditto without Honors.
.	547	734	414	100	67	100	312	70	571	50	100	Total Percentage passed.
												(Over Age).
.	.	.	.	.	.	4	.	1	.	.	1	Passed with Honors.
.	2	1	1	.	.	1	1	6	10	.	.	,, without Honors.
.	1	6	1	.	.	.	.	1	2	.	.	Failed.
.	0	3	2	.	.	1	6	8	13	.	1	Total Examined.
.	.	.	.	.	.	60	.	77	.	100	Proportion per cent who passed with Honors.	
.	457	332	67	.	.	50	30	573	757	.	.	Ditto without Honors.
.	457	374	60	.	.	137	60	612	541	.	100	Total Per-centage passed.

D

TABLE IV.—Showing for each subject (1) the number of students who passed failed, and (4) the total number examined; also the proportion and (6) who passed

GIRLS.

Total in all Grades (Of the Prescribed Age).		Subjects.											
	Greek	Latin	English	Commercial English	French	Commercial French	German	Commercial German	Italian	Commercial Italian	Spanish	Commercial Spanish	Celtic	Arithmetic
Passed with Honors	16	143	119	13	558	12	312	3	11	3	3	3	9	115
„ without Honors	15	588	1,275	16	762	30	169	9	51	1		1	7	687
Failed	8	729	283	17	644	16	143	1	29					670
Total Examined	55	688	2,676	62	2,065	61	662	14	143	1	3	7	16	1,322
Proportion per cent. who passed with Honors	46	272	278	216	113	273	472	272	364	76	167	160	462	241
Ditto, without Honors	676	119	378	634	309	334	320	67	313	26			53	284
Total Percentage passed	606	641	361	678	704	646	877	373	677	167	160	100	167	67
(Over Age.)													
Passed with Honors			38	1	29		8		3					31
„ without Honors	1	4	63	1	73	6	13	1	6					50
Failed		6	39	3	60	1	8							30
Total Examined	1	10	132	4	162	6	29	1	9					116
Proportion per cent. who passed with Honors			271	161	263		276		46					267
Ditto without Honors	167	40	424	360	463	64	473	167	67					417
Total Per-centage passed	167	64	762	67	762	64	743	167	167					672

with Honors, (2) the number who passed without Honors, (3) the number who per cent. to those examined of those who (5) passed with Honors, without Honors—*continued.*

GIRLS.

													Total in all Grades (Of the Prescribed Age).
Book-keeper	Euclid	Algebra	Algebra and Arithmetic	Plane Trigonometry	Natural Philosophy	Chemistry	Botany.	Drawing.	Music.	Domestic Economy.	Shorthand.	Plain Writing.	
60	120	134	10	9	3	3	20	644	163	611	16	7	Passed with Honors.
60	234	360	19	11	71	7	60	709	345	629	16	9	„ without Honors.
60	350	390	63	11	.	1	63	588	270	386	20	.	Failed.
120	654	1,160	61	61	14	10	117	1,831	715	2,106	60	9	Total Examined.
10	349	604	176	8	8	20	603	364	364	193	25	778	Proportion per cent. who passed with Honors
675	609	343	373	374	6	70	576	457	674	607	30	277	Ditto, without Honors
576	571	647	673	674	100	90	674	615	6	761	60	100	Total Per-centage passed.
													(Over Age).
4	8	7	.	.	.	.	.	13	11	10	.	9	Passed with Honors.
14	19	16	9	1	.	.	4	60	67	13	1	.	„ without Honors.
6	9	13	1	1	1	.	1	23	16	61	1	.	Failed.
63	34	61	9	7	1	.	5	99	99	164	9	9	Total Examined.
374	69	69	.	.	.	.	.	97	148	77	.	110	Proportion per cent. with passed with Honors.
674	603	60	97	66	.	.	60	373	379	60	60	.	Ditto, without Honors.
6	613	679	697	66	.	.	60	666	676	617	60	100	Total Per-centage passed.

TABLE V.—Showing the number of Students to whom £50 Prizes (Senior Grade), and Exhibitions were awarded.

	Senior Grade, £50.	Middle Grade, £30 tenable for two years.	Junior Grade, £20 tenable for three years.	Preparatory Grade, £20 tenable for one year.	TOTAL.
Boys, . . .	10	34	171	161	394
Girls, . . .	10	17	63	44	134
Gross Total, .	20	51	234	204	528

TABLE VI.—Showing the number of Students to whom Prizes in Books were awarded.

	First Class Prizes.	Second Class Prizes.	Third Class Prizes.	Total.
BOYS:—				
Preparatory Grade,* . .	—	—	131	164
Junior „ . .	34	48	71	137
Middle „ . . .	15	19	23	57
Senior „ . . .	8	8	18	34
Total, . .	57	76	263	402
GIRLS:—				
Preparatory Grade,* . .	—	—	58	58
Junior „ . . .	10	19	37	66
Middle „ . . .	3	5	20	28
Senior „ . . .	4	7	10	21
Total, . .	26	31	96	153
Gross Total, . .	83	107	384	584

TABLE VII.—Showing the number of Students to whom Prizes in
Composition were awarded. (Rule 52.)

	Greek	Latin	English	French	German	Italian	Celtic	Spanish	Total
Boys:—									
Preparatory Grade, 42,	8	7	7	4	2	3	7	–	24
Junior " 42,	5	8	9	6	3	2	0	–	40
Middle " 43,	8	1	3	4	4	1	1	–	20
Senior " 44,	3	3	3	3	4	1	3	–	17
Total,	17	14	23	19	14	8	13	–	113
Girls:—									
Preparatory Grade, 42,	–	1	–	4	5	–	–	–	16
Junior " 42,	2	3	3	8	0	1	–	–	18
Middle " 43,	–	–	2	6	8	–	–	1	11
Senior " 44,	–	–	4	3	4	–	–	1	12
Total,	2	4	9	16	18	2	–	1	52
Gross Total,	19	23	31	35	32	10	16	1	165

TABLE VIII.—Showing the number of Students to whom Special
Commercial Prizes were awarded. (Rule 48.)

	Number.	Value.
Boys:—		£
Junior, £15,	8	90
Do., £10,	15	150
Do., £5,	7	35
Middle, £10,	–	–
Do., £5,	1	5
Total,	39	280

TABLE IX.—Showing the number of Students to whom Medals were
awarded. (Rule 49.)

	LARGE GOLD MEDALS.	SMALLER GOLD MEDALS.				
GRADE.	First in Grade.	First in Classics.	First in English.	First in Mathematics.	First in Modern Languages.	
Boys, Senior,	1	1	*1	1	1	
Middle,	1	1	1	1	1	
Junior,	1	1	1	1	1	
Girls, Senior,	1	–	–	*1	1	
Middle,	1	–	–	1	1	
Junior,	1	1	1	*1	1	
Total,	6	4	3	4	6	

* In each of these cases the Student, being disqualified for award of a second Medal (Rule 49, part 3), have been awarded a Money Prize of £4.

TABLE X.—ACCOUNTS of the BOARD (original

(A) CAPITAL

	Securities.			Cash.		
	£	s.	d.	£	s.	d.
Balance on 1st January, 1897,	1,028,538	10	1	—		
Surplus Income (from Income Account),	—			4,063	8	2
Securities purchased, viz. :—Government 2½ per cent. Stock,	4,431	1	7	—		
Cash proceeds of Securities Sold,	—			1,576	13	0
£	1,032,969	11	8	6,539	0	3

(B) INCOME

Receipts.	£	s.	d.	£	s.	d.
In respect of the year 1896 :—						
Cash Balance as per Report of 1896,	5,769	4	11			
Income Tax refunded,	1,063	0	8			
Results Fees refunded, 1905,	8	15	0			
Locomotive Expenses refunded,	1	1	7			
Writer's Pay refunded,	0	4	0			
Petty Expenses refunded,	0	1	0			
				6,850	13	2
[Cr. Balance, 1896, £6,445 10s. 8d.]						
In respect of the year 1897 :—						
Interest on Securities,	25,189	4	8			
" on Cash on deposit,	60	18	0			
Examination Fees,	1,156	18	8			
Do. (late) Fees,	12	15	0			
Sale of Waste Paper,	0	13	8			
Sale of Publications,	143	1	7			
				30,550	8	7
Cash proceeds of Securities Sold,				1,575	13	0
* [Dr. Balance, 1897, £507 11s. 0d.]						
				£ 38,983	8	8

* There is a tax liability, in addition to this Balance, estimated at £246.

Endowment) for the year ended 31st December, 1807.
ACCOUNT.

	Former Offce. £ s. d.	Cash. £ s. d.
Cash invested in Government Securities (as per contra),	—	4,963 8 2
Securities held,	1,400 0 0	1,575 19 0
Balance on 31st December, 1897,	1,031,509 11 8	—
£	1,033,909 11 8	6,539 0 2

ACCOUNT.

PAYMENTS.		£ s. d.	£ s. d.
In respect of the year 1896:—			
Administration—			
Incidentals,		71 0 9	
Printing and Stationery,		31 8 10	
Cost of Audit,		100 0 0	
			108 18 7
Examinations—			
Printing and Stationery,		194 8 6	
Petty Expenses,		0 12 6	
Minor Prizes,		11 8 0	
			911 17 11
In respect of the year 1897:—			
Administration—			
Permanent Salaries,		3,899 18 0	
Writers,		340 6 8	
Rent,		64 18 4	
Printing and Stationery,		65 18 2	
Incidentals,		290 0 8	
			4,180 10 10
Examinations—			
Examiners' Remuneration,		6,085 0 0	
Do., Locomotive Expenses,		80 1 6	
Do., Incidental and Petty Expenses,		10 4 1	
Central Superintendents' Remuneration,		3,884 0 0	
Do., Locomotive Expenses,		186 11 6	
Do., Incidental and Petty Expenses,		358 12 7	
Hire of Rooms,		304 1 0	
Printing and Stationery,		1,314 7 9	
Petty Expenses,		790 3 8	
Locomotive &c.,		10 10 0	
			18,802 4 10
Prizes &c.—			
Money Prizes and Exhibitions, 1897 (new Awards),		4,251 0 0	
Retained Exhibitions of 1895 and 1896,		1,850 0 0	
Results Fees,		7,063 6 4	
Medals and Minor Prizes,		979 9 9	
			14,193 16 1
Miscellaneous—			
Income Tax to be refunded,		—	943 10 8
Law Costs,		—	16 19 2
On account of Surplus Income (transferred to Capital Account),		—	4,963 8 2
Balance,		—	671 17 6
		£	39,981 8 9

* All Expenses of Administration and Examination are paid out of the original Endowment of the Board, payments from the Local Taxation Grant being limited to Results Fees and rewards to Students.

TABLE XII.—THE "BURKE MEMORIAL FUND"

Account for the Year ended 31st December, 1897.

CAPITAL ACCOUNT.

Consols 1½ per cent. Consols, £1,233 13s. 11d. | Balance at Dec. 31, 1897, . . £1,233 13s. 11d.

	£	s.	d.			£	s.	d.
Balance on 1st January, 1897, . .	1	7	6	Prizes (while page n.), ...	8	0	0
„ Less, Quarter's Dividend at 1½ per cent. Consols,	8	8	9	Printing and Stationery, . . .	0	13	4
„ April, ...	8	8	9	Balance on Dec. 31, 1897, .	1	0	9
„ July, ...	8	8	9				
„ Oct.	8	8	9				
	£9	0	1		£9	0	1

Given under our Common Seal

this 9th day of March, 1898.

(L. S.)

Present at Board Meeting when Seal was affixed,

T. J. BELLINGHAM BRADY, } *Assistant Commissioners.*
JOHN C. MALET,

NAMES OF THE COMMISSIONERS

OF

INTERMEDIATE EDUCATION (IRELAND).

The Right Hon. CHRISTOPHER PALLES, LL.D., Lord Chief Baron of
the Exchequer in Ireland, Chairman.
The Right Hon. Mr. Justice MADDEN, Vice-Chairman.
The Rev. GEORGE SALMON, D.D., D.C.L., LL.D., F.R.S., Provost, Trinity
College, Dublin.
The Right Hon. O'CONOR DON, H.M.L., LL.D.
Rev. W. TODD MARTIN, D.D., D.LIT.
DAVID C. BARKLEY, Esq., LL.D.
His Grace The Most Rev. WILLIAM J. WALSH, D.D., Archbishop
of Dublin.

ASSISTANT COMMISSIONERS.

T. J. BELLINGHAM BRADY, M.A., LL.D.
JOHN C. MALET, M.A., F.R.S.

APPENDIX I.

LIST of PERSONS from whom the Examiners for 1807 were
selected, with the approval of the LORD LIEUTENANT
(Rule 0).

GREEK AND LATIN.

Armour, Rev. James R., M.A. (Q.U.I.)
Barrett, Rev. R.
Benre, John T., M.A., F.T.C.D.
Bryce, A. Hamilton, LL.D.
Bury, John D., M.A. (Dub.), F.T.C.D.
Butler, Edward G., Sen. Mod., T.C.D.
Butler, Rev. M. J., D.A., D.D.
Carleton, Rev. James G., B.D., Sen. Mod., T.C.D.
Cowan, Arthur, M.A. (R.U.I.), B.A. (Dub.), Sen. Mod., T.C.D.
Cotter, W. E. P., B.A., 1st Sen. Mod., T.C.D.
Crowe, Rev. Jeremiah, St. Patrick's College, Thurles.
Dickey, Rev. R. H. F., M.A., B.D.
Dickie, John, B.A. (Dub.), 1st Sen. Mod., T.C.D.
Dougan, T. W., M.A., Ex-Fellow, St. John's College, Cambridge,
  Professor of Latin, Queen's College, Belfast.
Dowdall, Rev. Launcelot D., LL.B. (Dub.), M.A. (Oxon.), 1st Sen Mod.,
  T.C.D., University Student.
Doyle, Charles F., M.A. (F.R.U.I.), B.A. (Dub.), Sen. Mod., T.C.D.
Doyle, Robert, B.A. (Dub.), Moderator, T.C.D.
Exham, Gerard, M.A., F.T.C.D.
Golligher, W. A., M.A., Sen. Mod., T.C.D.
Gorham, Alfred, B.A. (Dub.) Sen. Mod., T.C.D.
Hamilton, Rev. A. B., M.A., LL.B. (R.U.L.)
Hayes, Rev. Laurence J., D.D., Professor, St. Patrick's College, Thurles.
Healy, John, B.A.
Hitchcock, Rev. Francis R. M., M.A., B.D., Dub., 1st Sen. Mod., Univ.
  Student, T.C.D.
Keane, Charles, M.A. (Dub.), Professor of Greek, Queen's College, Cork.
Kelly, Very Rev. J. J., Canon.
Kennedy, Wm., M.A., Univ. Student (R.U.I.), B.A. (Dub.), Sen. Mod., T.C.D.
Kerin, R. C. B., B.A., 1st Class Classical Honours, London.
Maguire, Rev. E., D.D.
Mannix, Rev. D., Professor, St. Patrick's College, Maynooth.
Marshall, Rev. P., Professor, Ecclesiastical College, Carlow.
M'Glone, Rev. Peter, D.D.
M'Neill, Hugh A., B.A. (R.U.I.)
M'Rory, Rev. Joseph, D.D., Professor, St. Patrick's College, Maynooth.
Molohan, John P., M.A. (Dub.), Sen. Mod., T.C.D.
Montgomery, Robert, M.A., University Student (R.U.I.), B.A., 1st Class
  Classical Tripos, Cantab.
Montgomery, Malcolm, M.A. (Dub.), 1st Sen. Mod., T.C.D., Univ. Student.
Morrissoe, Rev. Patrick, The College, Maynooth.
Newsome, Clarence, M.A. (R.U.I.), Sen. Mod., T.C.D.
O'Dea, Henry, B.A. (Dub.), Mod., T.C.D., M.A. (R.U.I.)
O'Farrell, Very Rev. J., Canon.
O'Neill, Rev. James.
Palmer, Arthur, M.A. (Dub.), F.T.C.D., Prof. of Latin, Univ. of Dublin.
Pulton, Rev. Samuel, M.A.
Purser, Louis C., D.LITT., F.T.C.D.
Rice, Rev. James, B.D. (Dub.), Sen. Mod., T.C.D.

Ridgeway, William, M.A. (Dub.), Ex-Professor of Greek, Queen's College, Cork; Fellow, Gonville and Caius College; Disney Professor of Archaeology, Cambridge.
Roberts, Theodore M., M.A. (Dub.)
Rowan, William H., M.A., Univ. Student (R.U.I.)
Rutherford, H. E., M.A., LL.D.
Ryan, Rev. Innocent, Professor, St. Patrick's College, Thurles.
Sandford, Rev. Herbert, M.A., Sen. Mod., T.C.D.
Sandford, Philip George, M.A. (Dub.), Professor of Latin, Queen's College, Galway.
Starkie, W. J. M., M.A., F.T.C.D.
Thompson, D'Arcy W., M.A. (Cantab.), F.R.U.I., Professor of Greek, Queen's College, Galway.
Tyrrell, Robert Y., M.A., D.LITT. (Dub.), F.R.U.I., Professor of Greek, University of Dublin.
White, Dudley J., B.A. (Dub.)
Wilkins, Rev. George, M.A. (Dub.), F.T.C.D.
Wilson, Herbert, B.A. (Dub.), 1st Sen. Mod., T.C.D.

ENGLISH.

Allen, Henry J., B.A. (Dub.), 1st Sen. Mod., T.C.D.
Bailey, William F., B.A. (Dub.), 1st Sen. Mod., T.C.D.
Barlow, Jane.
Barry, Rev. Louis Ang., LL.D. (Dub.), 1st Sen. Mod., T.C.D.
Bastable, C. F., B.A. (Dub.), Prof. of Political Economy, Univ. of Dublin.
Boyd, Andrew, M.A. (R.U.I.)
Brown, Samuel Lombard, B.A. (R.U.I.)
Carmichael, Rev. Frederick F., LL.D. (Dub.)
Cherry, Richard R., M.A., LL.D. (Dub.)
Coghlan, Rev. Daniel, St. Patrick's College, Maynooth.
Colclough, John D.
Cooke, John, M.A. (Dub.), Professor, Church of Ireland Training College, Kildare-place.
Coyle, Marie L., M.A.
Coyne, William P., M.A. (R.U.I.)
Croly, D., M.A. (R.U.I.)
Cunningham, E. M.
Cusack, John.
Dixon, G. Y., M.A., T.C.D.
Dixon, W. M., B.A., LL.B., 1st Sen. Mod., T.C.D.
Donnellan, Rev. James, St. Patrick's College, Maynooth.
Donovan, R., B.A. (R.U.I.)
Evans, Rev. Henry, D.D.
Fetherstonhaugh, Godfroy, B.A. (Dub.), 1st Sen. Mod., T.C.D., Univ. Student.
Fitzgibbon, Henry M., M.A. (Dub.), Senior Mod., T.C.D.
Fitz Henry, William A., M.A., LL.D.
Fogarty, Rev. M., St. Patrick's College, Maynooth.
Gilliland, W. L., B.A., LL.D. (Dub.), Senior Mod., T.C.D.
Graham, Wm., M.A. (Dub.), Professor of Jurisprudence and Political Economy, Queen's College, Belfast.
Hardy, William J., LL.D. (Dub.), Sen. Mod., T.C.D.
Harrison, Thomas, B.A., LL.D. (R.U.I.)
Hayden, Mary, M.A., Junior Fellow (R.U.I.)
Henry, Rev. J. Edgar, M.A. (R.U.I.)
Hordman, John O., M.A., Sen. Mod., T.C.D.
Hogan, Patrick J., M.A.

Humphreys, Rev. John, B.A.
Hyde, Douglas, LL.D.
Joyce, P. W., LL.D., Ex-Professor, Board of National Education.
Joynt, Maud A. E., M.A. (R.U.I.)
Keane, A. H., D.A.
Kehoe, Daniel, B.A. (Dub.), Senior Mod., T.C.D.
Kingston, Eileen, B.A. (R.U.I.)
Lannox, P. J., B.A. (R.U.I.)
Lynter, Mary A., M.A. (R.U.I.)
Lynter, Thomas W., M.A. (Dub.), 1st Senior Mod., T.C.D. ; Librarian,
    National Library of Ireland.
M'Bride, Rev. J. H., B.A. (R.U.I.)
M'Donald, Rev. Walter, D.D., St. Patrick's College, Maynooth.
Macken, James J., B.A. (R.U.I.)
Magennis, William, M.A., F.R.U.I.
MacMullen, S. J., M.A. (R.U.I.), Professor of History and English Litera-
    ture, Queen's College, Belfast.
Macran, Rev. Frederick W., B.A. (Dub.), 1st Sen. Mod., T.C.D.
Macran, Henry S., M.A., F.T.C.D.
Maturin, Charles, D.A., LL.D.
Megaw, R. D., M.A., LL.B. (R.U.I.)
Mulcahy, Rev. Cornelius, Professor of English Literature, Maynooth
    College.
Murphy, James.
Murphy, Katharine, M.A., Junior Fellow (R.U.I.)
Nash, Rev. Francis L., M.A. (Oxon.)
Newcombe, Rev. J. D. E., B.A., D.D. (Dub.), Sen. Mod., T.C.D.
Nicolls, Archibald J., LL.B. (Dub.)
O'Leary, Rev. Patrick, D.D., St. Patrick's College, Maynooth.
O'Loan, Rev. Daniel, D.D., St. Patrick's College, Maynooth.
Osborne, E. K., M.A.
Park, John, M.A. B.LITT. (R.U.I.), F.R.U.I., Professor of Logic and Meta-
    physics, Queen's College, Belfast.
Quinn, M. T., M.A., Univ. of London.
Rainsford, Edwin G., B.A., Sen. Mod., T.C.D.
Rea, Rev. George T., M.A.
Redmond, Frederick, B.A. (Dub.), Sen. Mod., T.C.D.
Rolleston, T. W., B.A., T.C.D.
Rowley, James, M.A., Professor of Modern History and English
    Literature, Univ. College, Bristol.
Savage-Armstrong, George F., M.A. (Dub.), D.LITT., F.R.U.I. ; Professor of
    History and English Literature, Queen's College, Cork.
Semple, R. J., M.A.
Smyth, Rev. J. Paterson, B.A., LL.D. (Dub.), Sen. Mod., T.C.D.
Stanton, Lucy Vera.
Steele, L. Edward, M.A. (Dub.), Professor, Church of Ireland Training
    College, Kildare-place.
Story, Mary, M.A., University Student (R.U.I.)
Taylor, John F., B.A. (Dub.)
Wolland, Rev. Charles W., B.A. (Dub.), Sen. Mod., T.C.D.
Whelan, Rev. Denis, St. John's College, Waterford.
Whitty, R. O. I., M.A. (Dub.), Sen. Mod., T.C.D.
Wilson, Rev. Thomas B., M.A. (Dub.), 1st Sen. Mod., T.C.D.
Witherow, Rev. J. M., M.A. (R.U.I.)
Woodburn, Rev. George, M.A., Professor, Magee College, Londonderry.
Wright, A. R., B.A. (Dub.), 1st Senior Mod., T.C.D.

FRENCH.

Amours, F. J., B. ès L. French Master, Glasgow Academy.
Bacon, John W., M.A. (R.U.I.)
Barbier, Paul E. E., Lecturer, French Language and Literature, Univ. Coll., Cardiff, South Wales.
Barrère, A., Prof. of French, Royal Military Academy, Woolwich.
Boielle, James, B.A. (Paris).
Bné, Henry, B. ès L. (Univ. Gall.)
Butler, W. F., M.A., Prof. of Modern Languages, Queen's College, Cork.
Cogery, A., B.A., LL. (Paris), Examiner in French, Trinity Coll., London.
D'Auquier, Rev. E. C., M.A. (Cantab.)
D'Auquier, T. C.
Decoudun, Lydia.
Dupuis, Alexandre L., B.A.
Herman, Walter, M.A., PH.D.
Hogan, Rev. J. F., St. Patrick's Coll., Maynooth.
Junius, Elphège, Assistant Examiner in the University of London.
Lawson, James.
Ludwig, A., D.A. (Univ. Gallic).
M'Weeney, Edmond J., M.A., M.B. (R.U.I.)
Masson, J. F. P.
Migel, N., B. ès L.
Morgan, Rev. W. Moore, LL.D., (Dub.)
Nif, Otto C., M.A., London.
Oger, Victor, French Lecturer, Univ. Coll., Liverpool.
Spencer, Frederic, M.A., PH.D., Professor of Modern Languages, University College, Bangor.
Voegelin, A., B.A. (London).

GERMAN.

Buchheim, C. A., PH.D., Prof. of German in King's College, London.
Fischer, E. L.
Hager, Herman, PH.D.
Heinemann, N., Prof. of German, Crystal Palace School of Arts & Sciences.
Hennig, Curt, M.A.
Houston, Rev. J. D. C., B.A.
Lange, Frans, PH.D., Prof. of German, Royal Mil. Academy, Woolwich.
Meissner, A. L., PH.D., Prof. Modern Languages, Queen's Coll., Belfast.
Oswald, E., M.A., PH.D. (Goettingen), Instructor in German to the Royal Naval College, Greenwich.
Schlomka, C., M.A., PH.D.
Selss, Albert M., M.A., LL.D. (Dub.), Sen. Mod., T.C.D., PH.D., Professor of German, University of Dublin.
Steinberger, Valentine, M.A. (R.U.I.), Professor of Modern Languages, Queen's College, Galway.
Welss, A., M.A., PH.D., Professor of German, Royal Military Academy, Woolwich.

ITALIAN.

Morosini, Francesco.
Murphy, Rev. W. H., D.D.
O'Keeffe, Rev. Barth. A., D.D.
Ricci, Luigi, Prof. City of London College.

SPANISH.

Wheeler, Rev. Thomas, B.J.

CELTIC.

Connolly, William P., B.A.
Flannery, T.
Hogan, Rev. Edmund, S.J.
Hyde, Douglas, LL.D. (Dub.)
McCarthy, Rev. B., D.D.
McNeill, John.
Molloy, John, B. en L.
Murphy, Rev. James E. H., M.A., Professor of Irish, Univ. Dublin.
O'Duffy, Richard J., Hon. Sec., Society for the Preservation of the
    Irish Language.
O'Growney, Rev. Eugene, Professor, St. Patrick's College, Maynooth.
Olden, Rev. Thomas, M.A.

MATHEMATICS.

Alexander, J. J., M.A. (R.U.I.), M.A. (Cantab.)
Allman, George J., LL.D., D.SC., F.R.S., Ex-Professor of Mathematics,
    Queen's College, Galway.
Anglin, A. H., M.A. (R.U.I.), M.A. (Cantab.), F.R.S.S., Professor of Mathe-
    matics, Queen's College, Cork.
Barrett, Rev. Michael.
Bergin, William, M.A. (Dub.), Sen. Mod., T.C.D., Professor of Natural
    Philosophy, Queen's College, Cork.
Barnard, Rev. J. H., M.A., D.D. (Dub.), F.T.C.D.
Best, Richard, M.A.
Burnside, Wm. S., M.A. D.SC. (Dub.), F.T.C.D., Prof. of Mathematics,
    Univ. of Dublin.
Carroll, Rev. P. J.
Coates, W. M., M.A. (Dub.), M.A. (Cantab.), Sen. Mod., T.C.D., Fellow of
    Queen's College, Cambridge.
Culverwell, Edward P., M.A., F.T.C.D.
Dawson, H. G., B.A. (Dub.), 1st Sen. Mod., T.C.D., M.A. (Cantab.),
    Ex-Fellow of Christ's College, Cambridge.
Dilworth, W. J., M.A.
Dowling, E. Hughes, M.A., Math. Tutor, University College, Stephen's-
    green, Dublin.
Dowling, P. A. E., M.A. (R.U.I.)
England, John, M.A. (Dub.), Ex-Professor of Natural Philosophy,
    Queen's College, Cork.
Fry, M. W. Joseph, M.A. (Dub.), F.T.C.D.
Gibney, James J., M.A. (R.U.I.)
Graham, Christopher, M.A. (Dub. and Cantab.), 1st Sen. Mod., T.C.D.,
    Ex-Fellow, Gonville and Caius College, Cambridge.
Griffin, Gerald.
Griffin, Robert W., LL.D. (Dub.)
Inwood, Thos. W., B.A. (Lond.)
Johnston, J. P., M.A. (Dub.), Sen. Mod., T.C.D.
Johnston, Swift P., M.A. (Dub.), 1st Sen. Mod., T.C.D., Univ. Student.
Joly, O. J., M.A., F.T.C.D.
Kelleher, Stephen B., M.A. (R.U.I.)
Kelly, Patrick.
Larmor, Joseph, M.A. (R.U.I.), M.A. (Cantab.), Senior Wrangler, Fellow of
    St. John's College, Cambridge, F.R.S.
Leebody, John R., D.SC. (R.U.I.), Professor of Mathematics and Natural
    Philosophy, Magee College, Londonderry.

Lennon, Rev. Francis, D.D., Professor of Mathematics and Natural Philosophy, St. Patrick's College, Maynooth.
Lyster, Arthur E., M.A. (Dub.), Sen. Mod., T.C.D.
McClelland, J. A., M.A.
M'Weeney, Henry O., M.A. F.R.U.L., Sen. Mod. (T.C.D.)
Minchin, George M., M.A., F.R.S. (Dub.), Professor of Applied Mathematics, Royal Indian Engineering College, Cooper's Hill.
Moran, Rev Francis, M.A. (Dub.)
Nixon, R. C. J., M.A.
O'Dea, Rev. Thomas, Professor, St. Patrick's College, Maynooth.
Orr, Wm. M'F., M.A. (R.U.I.), Sen. Wrangler, Fellow of St. John's College, Cambridge; Prof. of Applied Mathematics and Mechanism, Royal College of Science, Ireland.
O'Sullivan, A. C., M.A. (Dub.), F.T.C.D.
Panton, Arthur W., M.A., D.SC. (Dub.), F.T.C.D.
Power, Rev. Thos. R., Professor of Mathematics, St. Patrick's College, Thurles.
Rambaut, Arthur A., M.A., D.SC., Astronomer Royal of Ireland.
Rea, James C., B.A. (R.U.L), Professor, Church of Ireland Training College, Kildare-place.
Roberts, Rev. W. R. Westropp, M.A. (Dub.), F.T.C.D.
Russell, R., M.A. (Dub.), F.T.C.D.
Smith, Charles, M.A. (R.U.I.), 1st Sen. Mod. (T.C.D.), Univ. Student.
Tarleton, Francis A., LL.D., D.SC. (Dub.), F.T.C.D.
Thrift, W. E., M.A., F.T.C.D.
Warren, Rev. Isaac, B.A.
Yates, James, B.A., Sen. Mod., T.C.D.

ARITHMETIC AND BOOK-KEEPING.

Dowd, Rev. James, B.A. (Dub.), Sen. Mod., T.C.D.
Bond, H. S.
Browne, J. J.
Ellis, Wm. F., M.A., LL.B. (Dub.), Local Gov. Auditor, Ireland.
Farrelly, Daniel.
Fitzpatrick, B., Prof. of Mathematics, Catholic Training Coll., Drumcondra.
Hughes, Rev. William, D.D. (Dub.)
Irwin, Ven. Charles K., D.D. (Dub.)
Keoghan, Rev. Patrick, B.A. (R.U.I.)
Macbeth, Rev. John, LL.D. (Dub.)
O'Brien, Edward T., Accountant, Mining Co. of Ireland.
O'Connor, George R.
Sutcliffe, Rev. Thomas, B.A. (Dub.)
Tristram, Rev. John W., M.A. (Dub.), Sen. Mod., T.C.D., Diocesan Inspector and Secretary, Diocesan Board of Education.
Warnock, Rev. W. J., B.A. (R.U.I.)
Whitton, Frederick A., Accountant, Representative Church Body.

NATURAL PHILOSOPHY.

Anderson, Alexander, M.A., Fellow of Sydney Sussex College, Cambridge, Professor of Nat. Phil., Queen's College, Galway.
Barrett, W. F., F.R.S.E., Professor of Physics, R.C.SC.I.
Brown, Wm., Demonstrator in Physics, Royal Coll. of Science, Dublin.
Burke, John, B.A., Sen. Mod., T.C.D.
Coffey, George, B.E. (Dub.), Sen. Mod., T.C.D.
Doherty, J. J., LL.D. (Dub.), Sen. Mod., T.C.D.

Fitzgerald, George F., M.A. (Dub.), F.R.S., F.T.C.D.
Johnston, Rev. John, M.A.
Johnston, Margaret K., M.A.
Joly, John, D.Sc., F.R.S.
Larmor, Alex., M.A. (R.U.L.), B.A. (Cantab.), Fellow of Clare Coll., Cambridge.
Moore, Hugh Kerr, B.A. (Dub.), 1st Sen. Mod., T.C.D.
Orum, John E., M.R. (R.U.I.), M.A., Ex-Professor of Mathematics, &c.,
   Univ. of Windsor, N.S.
Paul, John, B.A. (R.U.I.)
Preston, Thomas, M.A. (Dub.), F.R.U.I., Sen. Mod., T.C.D.
Scott, A. W., M.A. (Dub.), Professor of Physical Science, St. David's
   College, Lampeter, South Wales.
Stewart, John Hunter, M.A., F.R.U.I., M.Sc. (London); Professor of Experi-
   mental Physics, University College, Dublin.

CHEMISTRY.

Adeney, Walter E., F.I.C., A.R.C.Sci.
Bell, Chichester, M.B. (Dub.), Sen. Mod., T.C.D.
Campbell, John, M.B. (Dub.), F.R.U.I., Professor, University Coll., Dub.
Davy, Edmund W., N.A., M.D. (Dub.)
Dixon, Augustus E., M.B., F.C.S., Prof. of Chemistry, Queen's Coll., Cork.
Falkiner, Ninian M., B.A., M.CH. (Dub.), F.C.S.I.
Foy, P. Bertram.
Lapper, Edwin, L.K.Q.C.P.I., Lec. in Chem., Carmichael School of Medicine.
Lotts, Edmund A., PH.D., F.C.S., Prof. of Chemistry, Queen's Coll., Belfast.
Macnabb, John, Laboratory, Royal College of Surgeons, Ireland.
M'Hugh, Michael, M.B. (Dub.), Senior Mod., T.C.D.
Moss, Richard J., F.C.S., F.I.C., Registrar and Chemical Analyst, Royal
   Dublin Society.
Pratt, J. Dallas, M.A., M.D.
Reynolds, James Emerson, M.D. (Dub.), F.R.S., Professor of Chemistry,
   University of Dublin.
Robertson, Mary W., M.A. (R.U.I.)
Werner, Emil A., F.C.S.

BOTANY.

Anderson, R. J., M.A., M.D. (R.U.I.), Prof. of Nat. Hist., Queen's Coll.,
   Galway.
Blayney, Alexander, M.A., M.D.
Boulger, G. S., F.L.S., F.C.S.
Dixon, Henry H., B.A., Son. Mod., T.C.D.
Dunne, William, M.A.
Hartog, Marcus M., M.A., D.SC., F.L.S., Prof. Nat. Hist., Queen's Coll., Cork.
Malville, Alex. G., M.D. (Edin.), M.R.C.S.E., Ex-Professor of Natural
   History, Queen's College, Galway.
Pim, Greenwood, M.A. (Dub.), Sen. Mod., T.C.D.
Sigerson, George, M.D., M.CH. (R.U.I.)
Wilson, Andrew, PH.D., F.R.S.E., F.L.S.
Wright, Ed. Perceval, M.D. (Dub.), Prof. of Botany, University of Dublin.

DRAWING.

Atkinson, George M., Exm., Science and Art Department, South
   Kensington.
Bowler, H. A., Inspector and Assist. Director, Art Division, Science and

Conan, Florence.
Crabtor, Walter, Head Master, Government School of Art, Stevenson Memorial Hall, Chesterfield.
Crowther, W. E.
Harris, Robert, Art Master, St. Paul's School, London.
Jackson, Joshua, Art Master, Manchester Grammar School.
Keogh, Alice M.
Langman, A. W. F., Senior Drawing Inspector to the London School Board.
Lindsay, Thomas M., Drawing Master, Rugby School.
O'Brien, Edward Stewart, R.A., R.E. (R.U.I.)
Prendergast, P. J., A.M.I.C.E.
Rawle, John S., F.S.A.
Scully, T., R.E. (R.U.I.)
Vinter, J. A., London.

THEORY OF MUSIC

Allison, H., MUS.D. (Dub.)
Bowermnge, Rev. H., St. Patrick's College, Maynooth
Elliott, Stanislaus.
Garrett, George, MUS.D., M.A. (Cantab.)
Gator, William H., R.A., MUS.D. (Dub.)
Gick, Thomas, MUS.D. (Dub.)
Goodwin, W. G.
Haurafty, J. H.
Houghton, Edward.
Joze, T. R. G., MUS.D. (Dub.)
Kerbusch, L., MUS.D. (Dub.)
Malone, Robert, MUS.D. (Dub.)
Marks, J. Chr., MUS.D. (Oxon.)
Marks, T. Osborne, MUS.D.
Muntz, Ellis.
Patterson, Annie, MUS.D.
Rogers, Brendan J.
Seymour, Joseph, MUS.B.
Smith, Joseph, MUS.D. (Dub.)
Taylor, Charlotte M., MUS.B. (R.U.I.)

DOMESTIC ECONOMY.

Barrington-Ward. M. J., M.A. (Oxon.), H. M. Inspector of Schools.
Daly, Mary.
Gallaher, Fannie M.
Harrison, W. Jerome, Science Demonstrator, Birmingham School Board, &c.
McCarthy, Margaret.
Moore, Elizabeth.
Todd, Mary Bellingham.

SHORTHAND.

Doyle, M. F.
Bunbury, George William.
Healy. B. C. Wallis.

APPENDIX II.

LIST OF EXAMINERS

SELECTED, WITH THE APPROVAL OF THE LORD LIEUTENANT, TO
CONDUCT THE EXAMINATIONS IN 1887

GREEK AND LATIN.

Beare, John I., M.A., F.T.C.D.
Doyle, Charles F., M.A., F.R.U.I., B.A. (Dub.)
Hamilton, Rev. A. B., M.A., LL.B. (R.U.I.)
Maguire, Rev. Edward, B.D.
M'Neill, Hugh A., B.A. (R.U.I.)
Mulohan, John P., M.A. (Dub.)
Purser, Louis C., D.LITT., F.T.C.D.
Rutherford, H. R., M.A., LL.B. (R.U.I.)
Sandford, Philip George, M.A. (Dub.), Professor of Latin, Queen's Coll.,
    Galway.
Starkie, W. J. M., M.A., F.T.C.D.
Tyrrell, Robert Y., D.LITT., F.T.C.D.
White, Dudley J., B.A. (Dub.)

ENGLISH.

Barlow, Jane.
Carmichael, Rev. Frederick F., B.D. (Dub.)
Coghlan, Rev. Daniel, D.D., St. Patrick's College, Maynooth.
Colclough, John D.
Coyne, William P., M.A. (R.U.I.)
Fogarty, Rev. M., St. Patrick's College Maynooth.
Graham, William, M.A. (Dub.), Professor of Jurisprudence and Political
    Economy, Queen's College, Belfast.
Kingston, Eileen, B.A. (R.U.I.)
Lynton, Mary A., M.A. (R.U.I.)
MacMullan, S. J., M.A. (R.U.I.), Professor of History and English
    Literature, Queen's College, Belfast.
Magennis, William, M.A., F.R.U.I.
Mulcahy, Rev. Cornelius, Professor of English Rhetoric, St. Patrick's
    College, Maynooth.
Nicolls, Archibald, J., LL.B. (Dub.)
Park, John, D.LITT., F.R.U.I.
Savage-Armstrong, George F., D.LITT., F.R.U.I., Professor of History and
    English Literature, Queen's College, Cork.
Steele, L. Edward, M.A. (Dub.)
Taylor, John F., B.A (Dub.)
Whitty, R. C. I., B.M. (Dub.)

Butler, W. F., M.A., F.R.U.I., Prof. of Modern Languages, Queen's
College, Cork.
Janan, Elphege
M'Weeney, Edmond J., M.A. (R.U.I.)
Ogar, Victor.
Selss, Albert M., M.A., LL.D. (Dub), PH.D., Professor of German,
University of Dublin.
Spenser, Frederic, M.A., PH.D., Professor of Modern Languages, University
College, Bangor.

GERMAN.

Steinberger, Valentine, M.A., F.R.U.I., Professor of Modern Languages,
Queen's College, Galway.

SPANISH.

Wheeler, Rev. Thomas, S.J.

ITALIAN.

Ricci, Luigi.

CELTIC.

Hyde, Douglas, LL.D. (Dub.)

MATHEMATICS.

Allman, George J., M.A., LL.D. (Dub.), F.R.S. ; Ex-Professor of Mathe-
matics, Queen's College, Galway.
Bergin, William, M.A. (Dub.), Professor of Natural Philosophy, Queen's
College, Cork.
Bernard, Rev. J. H., M.A., D.D. (Dub.), F.T.C.D.
Dowling, P. A. E., B.A. (R.U.I.)
Griffin, Robert W., LL.D. (Dub.)
Inwood, Thomas W., B.A. (Lond.)
Johnston, J. P., M.A. (Dub.)
Kellaher, Stephen B., M.A. (R.U.I.)
Kelly, Patrick.
M'Weeney, Henry C., M.A., F.R.U.I.
Power, Rev. Thomas R., Prof. of Mathematics, St. Patrick's Coll.,
Thurles,
Rambant, Arthur A., M.A., D.Sc. (Dub.), Astronomer Royal of Ireland.
Tarleton, Francis A., LL.D., D.Sc., F.T.C.D.
Thrift, W. E., M.A., F.T.C.D.

ARITHMETIC AND BOOK-KEEPING.

NATURAL PHILOSOPHY.

Burke, John, B.A. (Dub.)
Scott, A. W., M.A. (Dub.), Professor of Physical Science, St. David's College, Lampeter, South Wales.

CHEMISTRY.

Adeney, Walter E., F.I.C., A.R.C.SC.L.

BOTANY.

Blayney, Alexander, M.A., M.B. (R.U.I.)

DRAWING.

Atkinson, George M., Examiner, Science and Art Department, South Kensington.
Langman, A. W. F., Senior Drawing Inspector to the London School Board.
Prendergast, P. J., A.M.I.C.E.
Scully, T., B.E. (R.U.I.)

THEORY OF MUSIC.

Marks, J. Chr., MUS.D. (Oxon.)

DOMESTIC ECONOMY.

Barrington-Ward, M. J., M.A. (Oxon.)
Gallaher, Fannie M.

SHORTHAND.

Holt, Henry.
Ryan, Charles.

APPENDIX III.

EXTRACTS FROM THE REPORTS OF THE EXAMINERS,
1897.

GREEK.

SENIOR GRADE.—FIRST PAPER.—BOYS.

Report of R. Y. TYRRELL, D. LITT.

In the Senior Grade the answering was satisfactory, the composition especially showing signs of improvement, so far as I can recollect my impressions of three years ago when last I examined.

The translation of the Odyssey was not better than might have been expected from senior boys having so short a course for the whole year's study. Part of the *De Corona* and one book of the *Odyssey* seems but a meagre year's work in Greek for a boy of eighteen.

There was only one question which was almost uniformly omitted or unsuccessfully attempted, I refer to question five on the use of certain combinations of particles, namely καὶ δή, καὶ μήν, μὲν οὖν, οὐκ οὖν, μὲν ἀλλά. This was a very definite question, and dealt with a subject excellently treated in many books on Greek syntax, a knowledge of which might well have been expected from candidates in the Senior Grade. Yet little or no instruction seems to have been given in this department of syntax so characteristic of the Greek language. Indeed one candidate seemed to resent the question, adding that in his opinion and that of other well-judging friends of his the whole four combinations meant much the same thing, and were never translated.

The answering in Grammar and scansion was good, the latter showing a decided improvement.

SENIOR GRADE.—SECOND PAPER.—BOYS.

Report of P. SANDFORD, M.A.

rendered "The cities were demoralised, some being bribed in their course of policy, . . while of the private citizens, &c." A senior grade boy while writing this down from memory should have felt it to be wrong, and the antithesis should have shown him the sense: "the cities were demoralised as the public men were corrupt and the private citizens lacking in foresight, or apathetic." The latter portion of C required delicate handling, as, in the words of one candidate, "it had to be broken up to avoid a load of dependent clauses." The *verbatim* rendering, even when given accurately, if not incorrect, was certainly inelegant.

The questions on the text and subject matter were, as a rule, satisfactorily answered.

The "night" passage from the *Odyssey* was attempted by nearly all, and with greater success than the prose passages. This latter, a piece of Aeschines' speech to which Demosthenes directly alludes, seems to have caused most of the candidates more difficulty than might have been expected. There were some marked exceptions, where the students evidently grasped the complete sense and failed only in the exact rendering of some words. The amount of weight attached to translation at sight ought to impress on teachers and learners the importance of a knowledge of Greek as compared with an acquaintance with a Greek book mainly acquired from translation. I would caution students against forcing a preconceived meaning into words, e.g., "will never value you more highly than strangers," rendered far too often for "will never value more highly you who are not related to him."

The History was carefully and minutely studied, and more attention was paid to the chapters on Literature and Art than formerly. There were very few complete failures. Most papers showed the precision, the neatness, and the intelligent use of knowledge acquired which one has learned to expect from candidates in the higher grades at the Intermediate Examinations.

SENIOR GRADE.—FIRST PAPER.—GIRLS.

Report of R. Y. TYRRELL, D. Litt.

The remarks made in the report on the boys of this grade are equally applicable to the girls, the general character of whose answering was much the same.

SENIOR GRADE.—SECOND PAPER.—GIRLS.

Report of P. SANDFORD, M.A.

There were not many papers sent in by girls, but these were sufficient to show that some of the Irish girls' schools teach Greek with intelligence and success. All the papers were fair, some were excellent, though none equalled the best among the boys. The remarks made in the report on the boys' answering on this paper apply equally to the girls.

MIDDLE GRADE.—FIRST PAPER.—BOYS AND GIRLS.

Report of JOHN P. MOLOHAN, M.A.

This paper consisted of questions on Grammar, sentences for translation from English into Greek, translation into English from Plato (Apology of Socrates) and questions arising out of the subject matter of the prescribed author.

The Grammar questions were answered fairly, especially those on the syntax; the questions which gave most trouble to the candidates were—strange to say—No. 1, on the declension of nouns, and No. 3, on the parsing and conjugation of verbs.

In many cases the sentences for composition, which were adapted from the Apology, were rendered into correct and idiomatic Greek, showing that the candidates had studied the prescribed author with thoroughness, and had not been satisfied with merely acquiring the translation. The candidates recommended for Composition prizes obtained from 80 to 87 per cent. of the total of the marks allotted to Composition.

The translation of the passages from the Apology was well done, though there were not wanting signs that a translation had been learnt by heart in some cases; ἀπόφασις in the text of Question 8 A. was in a few instances translated as if the reading were the alternative ἀπόφασις. The answers to the questions on the subject matter were not quite so satisfactory.

These remarks do not apply to the 'Over-age' Candidates, who were very weak in Grammar and Composition, and had, a good many of them, got off by rote the translation of 8 A. Passage 8 B. was known by comparatively few.

The girls, though none equalled the best of the boys, were a very even and good class. Their papers were models of neatness and good arrangement.

I would recommend candidates to answer the whole of a question together. In one case two pages of answers on Grammar and on the subject matter of the author separated different portions of the same piece of translation. It would be advisable to begin each answer on a separate page.

MIDDLE GRADE.—SECOND PAPER.—BOYS AND GIRLS.

Report of W. J. M. STARKIE, M.A.

The passages from the Hecuba were rendered with moderate accuracy. The general sense of the Greek was correctly given, but the more subtle points of scholarship were, for the most part, disregarded. The close—almost verbal—resemblance between the renderings of the majority of the candidates proves almost to demonstration that some inferior "crib" had been learned by heart, and that the students preferred to draw upon the storehouse of their memories than to straight and expeditious path of learning the Greek language rather than to strain their memories by overloading them with a mass of verbiage of less than no educational value.

The Grammar questions, though simple, seemed to present insuperable difficulties to a large proportion of the candidates. The use of *ἵνα* with the imperfect and aorist indicative (question 2 (b)), although fully explained in the edition of the *Hecuba* recommended by the Commissioners, was practically unknown to all.

The passages set for unseen translation were admirably rendered by the best scholars, but the weaker results fared less satisfactorily. The majority of the students were quite unable to keep a firm grasp on the sense of a consecutive passage, or to steer their way successfully through a long, though simple, Demosthenic period. The long-continued misuse of "cribs" has trained young scholars to translate *ped-temptim*, and to treat the matter of a passage or work as of no considerable importance. The study of an ancient literature conducted on such principles is positively injurious to the intellect. In fact, it may be said, without exaggeration, that a boy's brain is never in such a state of absolute passivity as when he has a translation in his hand. The historical questions were well answered. In this subject a marked advance has been made in recent years.

JUNIOR GRADE.—FIRST PAPER. BOYS AND GIRLS.

Report of JOHN P. MORGHAN, M.A.

That the girl candidates were exceptionally brilliant is shown by twelve candidates out of the thirteen examined obtaining "Honor" marks in Grammar and Composition combined. I wish to congratulate both the candidates and their teachers—the former on the great ability and careful study shown in their work, and the latter on the thorough and accurate manner in which their pupils have been taught.

JUNIOR GRADE.—SECOND PAPER.—BOYS AND GIRLS.

Report of W. J. M. STARKIE, M.A.

The passages from Lucian were, on the whole, well rendered. The scholarship shown was of a comparatively high order, and the English was not deficient in style. The chief difficulties were not slurred, and the large proportion of the candidates exhibited a praiseworthy desire to adhere to the sense of the Greek. In many cases, however, the examiner was tempted to surmise that a very inferior translation had been committed to memory, as identical blunders were committed by a long succession of candidates, and passages, bearing a superficial resemblance to the text, were substituted from other parts of the *Dialogues.*

The questions on Grammar elicited a plentiful crop of inaccurate information. Not more than 2 per cent. of the students have yet learned the parts of the verb "to die," that are normal in Attic Greek prose. It is an encouraging fact that the question on the matter of the book was answered by a large proportion of the candidates.

The historical knowledge exhibited in the answers to historical questions was both full and accurate. The life of Pericles was treated in a masterly way by many.

PREPARATORY GRADE.—FIRST PAPER.—BOYS AND GIRLS.

Report of P. SANDFORD, M.A.

PREPARATORY GRADE.—SECOND PAPER.—BOYS.

Report of R. Y. TYRRELL, D. LITT.

The translation of the passages from Xenophon was done excellently by most of the candidates, and only a very small percentage spelled Xenophon with a Z; which was gratifying, as I remember the time when this mistake in spelling was all but universal. The History, too, showed an improvement on what I remember of former examinations.

The parsing was not so good as might have been expected of carefully taught boys of from twelve to fourteen years of age. Hence the place for "translation at sight" was, as a rule, badly done. An inspection of the marking-sheet will show that as a rule when question 3 (asking for the accurate parsing of five verbal forms occurring in the prescribed book) was well answered, a more or less successful attempt was made to construe the unprescribed Greek, sometimes a very successful attempt indeed. The sentences were quite easy.

For instance, to enable a candidate to obtain full marks for 6(c) καὶ ἀφικνεῖται—Δαρεῖον, hardly anything was necessary but to know the meaning of three very common verbs, ἀφικνεῖσθαι, ἀπαγγέλλειν, and ξυλλαμβάνειν, and to recognise the form of each occurring in the passage. Two out of the three—all but ξυνελήφθη—were obvious: and it does not seem too much to expect even a candidate in the Preparatory Grade to know that εἴληφα is the perfect of λαμβάνω. It is amazing how few boys know the meaning of such common words as εἰσφέρομαι and σμικρὸν δεῦμα. In many cases, too, there seemed to be a complete ignorance of the relations of words towards each other in the sentence, though, perhaps, the same candidate might have translated quite rightly the passages set from the prescribed book.

PREPARATORY GRADE.—SECOND PAPER.—GIRLS.

Report of R. Y. TYRRELL, D. LITT.

There were only two female candidates, and both were absolutely ignorant of Greek, as the marking sheet will show.

LATIN.

SENIOR GRADE.—FIRST PAPER.—BOYS.

Report of LOUIS C. PURSER, D.LITT.

The Senior Grade boys were fair—a few quite excellent. The set passages were as usual very well done on the whole, notwithstanding their difficulty, a considerable number of boys translating the passages from the Odes of Horace with much taste and refinement. As to the compositions, what I say of the Middle Grade (*infra*) applies here also. It is strange how commonly ignorance of the difference between the active and the passive voice is displayed. Half the candidates I should say treated *facimus* as the perfect passive infinitive. Even by good students the concords were ruthlessly broken. There is on the whole a deficiency in ordinary vocabulary.

SENIOR GRADE.—FIRST PAPER.—GIRLS.

Report of LOUIS C. PURSER, D.LITT.

There is nothing special to be said as regards the girls. They are perhaps not quite so good all round as the boys, but their answering was decidedly meritorious. Their mistakes were pretty much the same as those of the boys. Both in large numbers translated *Tene* in *Tene torquerier* (Horace— Satires, ii., 8, 67) by "Hold"; and *jurgatur* in Satires, ii., 2, 100, by "he swears." None of the compositions of the girls were of first-class excellence, and there was no verse. The inability to quote the stanza beginning *Eheu fugaces* was a little surprising; only two out of the sixty-six did it accurately.

SENIOR GRADE.—SECOND PAPER.—BOYS.

Report of H. E. RUTHERFORD, LL.D.

The answering in this paper is, on the whole, very satisfactory. The translation of the passages from the prescribed course is very good all round, and the same may be said of the annotations. The translations at sight are in many cases excellent, while a few have reached a very high standard indeed.

The answering in History and Literature is very disappointing. In many cases, by a little attention to this important part of the course, the candidates might have considerably increased their total marks.

SENIOR GRADE.—SECOND PAPER.—GIRLS.

Report of H. E. RUTHERFORD, LL.D.

The answering, on a general view, is very fair. The passages for translation from the course are of average excellence all round, while some of them are remarkably good.

The answers to the questions on the prescribed book are not quite up to the mark; a noticeable feature being the number of poor, and often amusing, conjectures offered by candidates.

The translations at sight have in several cases attained a high standard of excellence. The majority of the students, however, have not gone beyond a fair average. In quite a number of cases the rules of grammar are violently handled in an attempt to make sense out of the passage.

More attention should be given to the History and Literature. The dates, however, have in many cases been given with remarkable accuracy.

MIDDLE GRADE.—FIRST PAPER.—BOYS.

Report of LOUIS C. PURSER, D. LITT.

written at all, though it is always treated by examiners with the utmost indulgence when attempted. The chief faults of the greater mass of compositions in both grades are—(1) grievous disregard of the concords, (2) ignorance of the difference between the active and the passive voice. It was also rare to find a boy or girl in the composition declining *alius* or *alter* rightly, though doubtless if either of these words had been set as a specific Grammar question it would have been answered correctly. Teachers would do well, in my opinion, if they never let a day pass without making some of their pupils write before the class sentences illustrating some one or more of the concords. It is the exception to meet with a boy or girl who does not in ten or twelve lines of Latin fail to make practical use of the rule that a verb should agree with its nominative case in *number*; still more rarely is a relative found agreeing with its antecedent in *gender*. It was curious that many students used the genitive after *oblivisci* in the short sentence, 7*b.*, " It is easier to forgive an enemy than forget an injury," but failed to do so in the last line of the passage for Latin prose.

Middle Grade.—First Paper.—Girls.

Report of Louis C. Purser, D.Litt.

The general average of tolerableness is better maintained among the girls than among the boys; but, as far as I could make out, there were only two really promising scholars among the girls. None of the compositions were exceptionally good; but all the set work was prepared with great steadiness and deliberation. The same faults which are noticeable in the boys' work for the most part appear also in that of the girls.

Middle Grade.—Second Paper.—Boys.

Report of H. E. Rutherford, LL.D.

The general answering in this paper is remarkably good. A considerable number of students, however, have not attempted any of the questions at all, and several only one or two questions.

The questions on the prescribed course have been answered with considerable accuracy, the translations in particular showing very careful preparation.

The translations at sight have reached, on the average, a high standard of excellence, while a few are remarkably good.

The answering in History is fair on the whole, and in many cases excellent.

Middle Grade.—Second Paper.—Girls.

Report of H. E. Rutherford, LL.D.

The answering of the candidates in this paper is fairly good. There are only a few who have reached a very high standard, and, on the other hand, there are very few who do not show a fair knowledge of the subjects.

While the translations from the prescribed book are satisfactory, the majority of the candidates have not been very successful with the annotation.

The translations at sight are often very good. The answering in History, while in many cases excellent, is, on the whole, rather below

JUNIOR GRADE.—FIRST PAPER.—BOYS AND GIRLS.

Report of R. Y. TYRRELL, D.LITT., JOHN I. BEARE, M.A., W. J. M. STARKIE, M.A., and D. J. WHITE, B.A.

We observe, with regard to the answering on this paper, that the average continues good, and high excellence marks the work of a large number of candidates. The composition was in many instances very well done. The prevailing faults are such as seem almost inseparable from the work of youth. Over-haste in preparation is too often evident. This fault is exhibited conspicuously in the translation from the prescribed author. As usual, however, all who have scamped, or crammed up, this part of the business have failed utterly at the *ordo* test, the value of which as a criterion cannot be exaggerated. An examiner feels as if he were throwing marks away when giving (as he does under the existing rules) full credit to the remaining translation of candidates who, by their attempts at the "parallel columns," have convinced him that they do not understand the sense of the individual words of the passage, but are in reality writing down from memory a version which they have learned by rote. This is done with almost incredible accuracy by many of the students—a practice which nothing except the *ordo* test can expose.

It appears to us that it would be wise if, in future, classical examiners were instructed to inflict a penalty on students who utterly fail at the required literal version, by mulcting them not only of the marks assigned for this, but also of all, or the greater portion of, the marks they might otherwise make in the remainder of their translation. The *ordo* test, with such modification, might be profitably extended to all grades alike.

JUNIOR GRADE.—SECOND PAPER.—BOYS.

Report of Rev. A. B. HAMILTON, LL.B., HUGH A. M'NEILL, B.A., and P. SANDFORD, M.A.

This paper dealt with one prescribed author (Virgil, Aeneid, Book I.), translation at sight, and Roman History. The mere translation of the passages from Virgil was well done, and for this question many students scored full marks or nearly full marks. At the same time a large number of these had nothing like a commensurate knowledge of Latin, if we are to judge from their attempts at unseen translation and the parsing of the Virgil. A painfully large proportion of boys gave admirable versions of the prescribed text, who showed only the faintest evidence of having received such instruction in Latin as can be considered of real value. The questions on parsing were poorly answered by the great majority. The knowledge of prosody was satisfactory, that is to say, about one half of the students scanned the lines set, and a respectable number received substantially full marks.

One striking fact was apparent regarding the translation at sight. Of the weaker candidates—viz., those who scored less than 35 per cent. on this section of the paper, most were more successful at the verse no marks in History. For this reason alone many otherwise admirable students failed to reach a high standard on the paper. It was disappointing to discover how few knew the meaning of terms so common as *dictator, legio, comitia, turma*. The attempts to trace the changes in the number of praetors consisted often of an enumeration of the more distinguished Roman names familiar to the student. When we consider that the programme in History was limited to a period of 80 years (B.C. 264 to B.C. 175), it would have been natural to expect a greater number of really good answers.

JUNIOR GRADE.—SECOND PAPER.—(IRISH.

Report of Rev. A. B. HAMILTON, LL.D.

Most of the girls had prepared the prescribed course carefully and translated with fair accuracy. It would, however, be desirable that the candidates should become accustomed to write better English and to pay more attention to grammatical corrections. It is a pity that a deserving student should expose herself to loss of marks by writing " But the boy Ascanius . . . . he shall fill," or by coining such an adjective as " scronising."

Points of Grammar and criticism evidently do not in girls' schools receive the importance which they deserve. Very few were able to give the modern name of the Hebrus, and the notes written on the words " Volvendis mensibus " in the line

Triginta magnos volvendis mensibus orbes
Imperio explebit

were painful to read. Most candidates explained the phrase as an " Ablative Absolute " for which they got just that amount of credit which their answer deserved.

By far the weakest part of the girls' work I found to be their scansion. Here, with a very few exceptions, good and bad students stood on a common level of incompetency. I was astonished to find that out of 299 girls only three recognised that in the line

Litora lactetur odiis Junonis iniquæ

the peculiarity consists in the lengthening by arsis of the last syllable of *lactetur*. I presume that the obtuseness which remains blind to this obvious peculiarity is due to the deplorable neglect of verse-making in our Irish schools.

The unseen passages on the paper were translated by some of the girls with remarkable accuracy and correctness, one candidate having

PREPARATORY GRADE.—FIRST PAPER.—BOYS AND GIRLS.

Report of JOHN I. BEARE, M.A., and CHARLES F. DOYLE, M.A.

The answering of candidates on this paper has been very satisfactory. It presents, in substance, no features of special interest; but, as regards its form, we may mention a fact or two.

Many candidates whether from want of practical instruction, or from thoughtlessness, omit to number their answers. A great many also, for whatever reasons, distribute fragments of answers over their answer books in widely different places. Both these irregularities should be avoided. They create for an examiner a certain liability to overlook, and therefore not to mark, parts of the student's work. If students put in their answers in this careless and unmethodical way, some mistakes may possibly be made which would otherwise never occur. Even the most scrupulously careful examiners are human, and students should not increase their liability to error by the practice here referred to.

The answers of the girls call for little remark which does not also apply to those of the boys. In translation of English sentences into Latin, however, the latter have been, this year, decidedly superior

---

PREPARATORY GRADE.—SECOND PAPER.—BOYS.

Report of Rev. E. MAGUIRE, D.D.

The very best answer-books on this paper were not singularly brilliant; the number of blanks and obvious failures was unusually small; but the conspicuous feature was the creditable standard attained by the great bulk of the examinees. Bad spelling is an evil not easily overcome by children under fourteen years of age; incorrect punctuation is to be expected; capital letters are sometimes found ridiculously out of place. Yet the instances of gross and persistent misspelling, of total neglect of punctuation, and of erroneous interchange of small and capital letters, were surprisingly few.

It is a safe general rule that beginners ought to be taught to commence the translation of each distich of Ovid's Elegiacs by a change of paragraph and a capital letter marking the first word; but the not uncommon practice of teaching them to translate each verse in that way, has not the sanction of either usage or common sense.

All round, the answering in Roman History was not as good as might be fairly expected; a very small percentage of the candidates knew anything about the Third Macedonian War. The question in Prosody was satisfactorily solved by more than half the candidates.

It is a common experience to encounter instalments of an answer on portions of three or four non-consecutive pages. Such disconnected, piecemeal, half answer and half afterthought is a bewildering puzzle to the examiner. This practice or device could be easily suppressed by careful training.

While the two extremes of distinction and failure are less striking than in former years, the average answering has attained a notably higher level

PREPARATORY GRADE.—SECOND PAPER.—GIRLS.

Report of HUGH A. M'NEILL, B.A.

I have examined the answers of the girls on this paper, dealing with one prescribed author (Ovid, Selections), translation at sight and History. I was especially struck by the fact that the girls who answered well on the prescribed author and the translation at sight, thus promising to reach a very high total on the paper, appeared to neglect the History altogether. With very few exceptions good marks in History were obtained only by those who were extremely weak in Latin.

I take it to be an examiner's duty in his report to dwell rather on the imperfections than the merits of candidates, for the information of teachers among whom the report is circulated. In that light the following remarks are to be interpreted.

The parsing of the Ovid was indifferently done in most instances. In the line " *Nam dedit e specula rustica ubi signa tenentur*," it requires little knowledge of syntax to see that *signa* is the only word that can be the direct object of *dedit*, and in fact practically all the candidates so translate it. Yet when asked to "explain in what case *signa* stands and why," the majority do not attempt an answer, while of the remainder quite one-half say it is dative case. The translations of the prescribed text show that in schools sufficient attention is not paid to construing, although it is hard to see how children can acquire any reasonable facility in Latin without it. An examiner can here discover the first signs of that divorce between the study of Latin authors and Latin syntax which assumes a more formidable aspect in the higher grades. At this elementary stage one would think that syntax should scarcely be taught as a separate study beyond what is fundamentally necessary to make the connection of words in a Latin sentence intelligible. If teachers would make their lessons in syntax go hand in hand with the reading of the text much confusion would be avoided. For the sentence "*Traduntur ducibus moenia nuda suis*," I repeatedly found in the same answer book the translation "the walls stripped of their leaders," &c., and the explanation "*ducibus* = indirect object on *traduntur*," or "dative on *traduntur*" and the like. Less often was the translation "are delivered over to the leaders" with "*ducibus* ablative on *nudis*." Clearly what is wanted is to make syntax a living, practical study, useful mainly as an aid to reading, not an isolated system of abstract truths,—identified with the "whole existence" of Latin, not forming "of its life a thing apart."

The defects in the translation at sight were chiefly such as might be inferred from the preceding observations. One thing is noticeable, the girls are more adventurous than the boys in assailing the unknown. In fact there are few gaps or dashes in their answers.

Little remains to be said about the Roman History. Weakness was most apparent in the explanations of words arising in this connection. Perhaps it is too much to expect much knowledge of prosody in students so young. The most frequent answer to the direction to mark the feet and the quantity of the syllables in two given lines was:—"First line, 16 syllables; second line, 13 syllables."

I have not attempted to enlarge upon the many excellent papers received, especially meritorious in the matter of unseen translation.

ENGLISH.

Senior Grade.—First Paper.—Boys.

Report of WILLIAM MACENZIE, M.A.

The essays of the senior boys were very inferior. With the exception of some ten or fifteen, the best of them could lay claim to merely negative merits: they were fairly commonplace in matter; they violated the ordinary rules of Grammar but seldom; their punctuation was almost tolerable, and their spelling only at times was execrable. So far as literary quality is concerned, too many essays were simply beneath contempt.

This falling off is very remarkable. In previous years I was much struck with the number of really excellent compositions in the Senior Grade; this year I was startled by the uniform poverty of thought, and the uniform slovenliness of expression. It is to be feared that some of the schools from which these candidates entered, pay no proper heed to the teaching and practice of English Composition. Their neglect of this most important department of mental cultivation is probably responsible for the failure of the students to appreciate the prescribed play as a piece of literature.

The grammar portion of the paper consisted of four questions: one dealing with the history of the language; one with analysis of sentences; another with prosody; and a fourth with specialities of idiom and construction illustrated in phrases from "Macbeth." The history question and that on analysis were in nearly every case attempted, and frequently full marks were awarded to the answers. Knowledge of Prosody, however, was confined for the most part to the few who scored well in the "Macbeth" section of the paper—some of them, I was glad to note, were able to exhibit the metrical structure of the Sonnet by quoting in full and with perfect accuracy, the masterpieces of Milton and of Wordsworth. As regards the question dealing with special features of Grammar, the ignorance displayed by the candidates was amazing. Not five per cent of them could write a proper note on the phrases from Shakespeare: very many condemned the construction in "as who should say," correcting (!) it to "as men should say"; while others blandly explained that Shakespeare never fully understood English Grammar.

Senior Grade.—First Paper.—Girls.

Report of WILLIAM MACENZIE, M.A.

The report I have to make on the Senior Grade Girls is substantially the same as that which I have made on the Senior Boys.

The compositions were in nearly every case vapid and weak: even the best of them seldom rose above respectable mediocrity. The Grammar answers betrayed a lamentable lack of study and thought. In this section only the question on Prosody was generally answered with any degree of fulness and accuracy. "Macbeth" was apparently neglected in the schools this year; only a few girls showed any knowledge of the play as a piece of literature; the vast majority gave meagre and scrappy answers where the exercise of any faculty higher than memory was called for.

It is not an exaggeration to say that no more than twenty candidates gave evidence of having undergone efficient training for this examination.

————

SENIOR GRADE.—SECOND PAPER.—BOYS.

Report of JOHN PARK, D.LITT.

I read the answers of 303 boys to the second English paper, Senior Grade.

The answering was, I believe, as good as I had in 1804, regard being had to the fact that this year my papers were seconds, and had not the force and the freshness of morning work. One boy made the excellent total of 610 marks out of 650.

Bacon's *Selected Essays* had been carefully, and as a rule intelligently, prepared, and the marking was good and often very high. If Bacon had been well learned, the History seemed most known, especially the history of England; the 7th question which asked with what Irish art was concerned, and when it degenerated and why, gave free play to some wild freaks of wit and fancy :—

"The cultivation of the potato; Irish woollens; Irish linens; Irish lace; from the very earliest times; at the death of St. Patrick; at the Reformation; at the time of Cromwell; at the introduction of Christianity."

The Geography was not well made up, as senior candidates have much other work which they probably regard as of greater importance; and the answering in English Literature was best and least. The *Adonais*, ex. gr., was said to be written by Keats, Milton, Landor, Southey, Clarendon, Lamb, Pope, Wordsworth, and Spencer; and *Gulliver's Travels* was ascribed to Goldsmith, Defoe, and John Bunyan, "Gulliver is supposed to be a Christian travelling to different countries."

The writing, spelling, punctuation, and arrangement were usually good and often very neat and even elegant. I noticed here, and more frequently in the junior work, bits that seemed intended to pass the time till the examination was over; some made little puns on the name Bacon, and sprightly sallies—ex. gr., one said he didn't know where Manitoba, New Brunswick, and Rhode Island were, nor did he suppose it mattered to any one, as he had heard that all those places had been swallowed up by an earthquake last week!

SENIOR GRADE—SECOND PAPER—GIRLS.

Report of JOHN D. COLLOUGH.

The impression left upon my mind after examining 150 papers (Senior Grade—Girls—Second Paper) is one of some disappointment. Mediocrity both of thought and of expression is the characteristic of the greater number; not 15 per cent. reach a point of remarkable merit; while fully 30 per cent. sink below passing point on this paper.

The subjects were *Bacon's Essays* (selected), *Outlines of English Literature from 1674 to 1832*, *Geography*, and the *History of England and Ireland from A.D. 1714 to A.D. 1837*. I shall deal with these subjects separately.

A. I cannot say that the Bacon is not known. But I can say that the knowledge of the great writer, as displayed upon too many of these papers, is inaccurate and ill-digested. In many cases erroneous views, and in a few cases nonsense absolute, are fathered upon the philosopher. With the *soul* of the text, with that true inner significance of it which is best obtained by efficient oral exposition, too many of these papers record but a superficial acquaintance. The first question was—

1. In what connexion, and with what view, does Bacon use the following expressions?—

(a.) "The solecism of power";
(b.) "The helmet of Pluto";
(c.) "Keep the plough in the hands of the owners."

Now instead of (1) correctly quoting the title of the Essay from which (a), (b), and (c) are respectively taken; instead of (2) quoting the passage or sentence in which they respectively occur (or at least reproducing its substance); and instead of (3) explaining in brief and simple language the general drift of Bacon's meaning, perhaps a moiety of the candidates were satisfied to (1) quote the wrong Essay, (2) misquote Bacon, and (3) give an incorrect explanation or no explanation at all.

To understand Bacon's Essays both requires and stimulates high thinking. High thinking means hard work, particularly for school-girls who regard it as dry thinking. And so there is evidence upon too many of these pages of an effort to evade thinking at all.

B. The bright feature of the papers was the Geography. The questions both in political and physical Geography were excellently answered by most: not a few nearing full marks. Here and there, however, Meridians of Longitude were confused with Parallels of Latitude.

C. The questions on Irish History were answered with remarkable fulness and accuracy by most of the candidates; in fact the failures here were very few; but the answering in English History was by no means so good.

5. Name, with dates and very brief exposition the battles subsequent to 1750 which were most influential in determining the fortunes of Canada, India, and the United States.

6. Mention some famous reforms, social or municipal, which mark the period 1760-1830.

In question 5, quite a large number of candidates wrote a list of insignificant battles and skirmishes which were not "most influential," while only a few remembered the Capture of Montreal and the Battle of Wandewash which *were*. In question 6 the word *social* and the word *municipal* might have been Arabic for all the notice that was taken of either.

D. The answering in Literature was respectable, but not brilliant. In this department, as in the history, there appears to be a tendency to rely on mnemonic mastery of the actual words of certain handbooks. This practice should be sternly discountenanced, as tending to suppress the power of high personal endeavour. Many girls (and boys) are quite content to be saved the trouble of thinking for themselves. Thus, whatever could be directly gleaned from handbooks was reproduced with accuracy; but whatever could be secured only indirectly, whether by hard searching or by inference, i.e., by personal effort of will and judgment, was very feebly given where it was given at all. Of such kind were 10 (*b.*), 11 (*b.*), 12 (*b.*)

> 10. (*b.*) Show, by examples, that in the reigns of William III. and Anne literary merit was a passport to the highest favours of the State.

> 11. (*b.*) Name four books, written during the period prescribed, which illustrate Irish life.

> 12. (*b.*) Name the most typical poet, and name also the most powerful prose writer, of (1) *English*, (2) *Irish*, and (3) *Scottish* birth, belonging to the latter half of the 18th century.

It is pleasant to be able to add that the spelling and general neatness were eminently satisfactory. But of punctuation some of the papers were almost as innocent as a Greek manuscript.

MIDDLE GRADE.—FIRST PAPER.—BOYS.

Report of R. C. I. WHITTY, M.A.

The subjects in which I examined were—(1) Composition ; (2) Grammar (including Parsing) and Analysis; (3) Milton (*Lycidas, Il Penseroso* and *L'Allegro*) ; and (4) Gray (*The Bard, The Elegy,* and *The Ode on Eton College*).

The subjects set for COMPOSITION were :—

A. Describe the plot of any work of fiction you have read.

B. "Ye gentlemen of England that live at home in ease,
Ah! little do ye think upon the dangers of the seas."

C. "Gay Hope is theirs by Fancy fed,
Less pleasing when possest."—(Gray: *Ode on Eton College*).

A large number of boys chose subject A, and some of the descriptions were very well written and formed quite pleasant reading. *Robinson Crusoe* was the favourite story, while *Scott* (especially *Ivanhoe*), and *Dickens* were well supported. Of contemporary novelists, Rider Haggard seemed most popular. The "penny-dreadful" type of novel claimed a few admirers—a blood-curdling and thrilling romance called *The Iron Pirate* being, apparently, a special favourite of this class.

The largest number wrote upon subject B; but the work upon this subject was, with few exceptions, decidedly poor. It was marred by high-sounding and inflated adjectives, sham sentiment and affected piety, and was marked by an almost total absence of ideas, whether borrowed or original.

The Essays written upon subject C were, as a rule, of a thoughtful character, and some of them attained to a high degree of merit. But many of them were, to a certain extent, spoiled by being too religious in their tone, partaking more of the nature of a sermon than of an essay. This fault (if it may be so called) was more noticeable with the girls than with the boys.

Some students made a curious mistake in reference to the word "plot" in the wording of subject A, taking it to mean "conspiracy," and accordingly writing narratives of the Gunpowder Plot, Titus Oates's Plot, and other famous historical conspiracies.

The spelling, generally speaking, was good, and bad grammatical mistakes were rare; but, on the whole, the compositions were not up to the standard that might reasonably be expected of Middle Grade students. About 35 per cent. of the candidates failed to obtain quarter marks, and only about 13 per cent. obtained half marks. Some half dozen or so of the compositions were totally irrelevant to any one of the prescribed subjects.

The GRAMMAR and PARSING were well done, and most of the candidates showed a satisfactory knowledge of the rules of ANALYSIS, although many of them failed to make the most of that knowledge, owing to carelessness and slovenliness in drawing out their schemes.

The MILTON was, on the whole, well and carefully prepared, and the answering in it left little to be desired. In explaining the meaning of the lines from *Il Penseroso*—

> " Where I may oft out-watch the Bear
> With thrice-great Hermes,"   (Q. 4 (b))

some few of the candidates took them as referring to the animal instead of to the constellation, and accordingly gave rather ludicrous explanations.

In answering Question 6 ("Quote the lines from *Lycidas* referring to St. Peter ") one very curious mistake (common to boys and girls), constantly recurred, namely, that "the *Pilot* of the Galilean Lake" was written "the *Pilate* of the Galilean Lake."

The GRAY seems to have been learned merely by rote by the majority of the candidates, as comparatively few of the answers display an acquaintance with the meaning of the lines. Question 9 ("Trace briefly in your own words the succession of thoughts and reflections in Gray's *Elegy* ") was badly answered all round, by girls as well as boys; and it was quite amazing how very few understood that it is to *himself* the poet refers in the last few stanzas of the *Elegy.*

The line, "Their furrow off the stubborn globe has broke" (Q. 10 (b)),
gave rise to the most extraordinary and varied collection of explanations. One set of answers treated "furrow" as a plough or some part
of a plough; another set, on the other hand, attached this meaning
to "globe." "Furrow" was also said to be "a scythe" and "a
threshing-machine," while "stubborn globe" was variously explained as
"a team of horses" (this was by a girl), "a blustering colt," "the
oxen which ploughed the land," "the badly trained oxen," and (funniest
of all) "a root of the turnip family which is very tough and hard to
break." Mistakes of this nature in connection with this particular
line (but, of course, all of them not so ludicrously absurd as the ones
just quoted), were to be met with in fully one-half of the answers, and
did not merely occur in isolated instances, as was the case in the
question on the Milton (Q. 8 (f)), spoken of above.

———

MIDDLE GRADE.—FIRST PAPER.—GIRLS.

Report of R. C. I. WHITTY, M.A.

For the subjects in which I examined, and for the subjects set for
composition, I beg to refer to the beginning of my report upon the
Boys.

The COMPOSITIONS of the girls were, on the whole, considerably better
than those of the boys. This was principally owing to the fact that the
former devoted more time to them, manifestly regarding the Essay as a
serious and important part of the examination, whereas the boys in
many instances left it to the last, and then, apparently, hurried it off in
some fifteen or twenty minutes.

The girls for the most part wrote upon the lines from Gray (subject C),
and many of them handled the subject with considerable judgment and
skill—the most striking defect being an excessive tendency to "moralise."

Not as many as I expected chose subject A, but, of those who did, a
fair proportion wrote in a pleasant and natural manner, giving the plots
of their stories graphically, lucidly, and concisely. They drew principally upon the works of the more modern authors—Scott and Dickens
having, apparently, very few admirers. "In the Mine," by Mrs. Henry
Wood, seemed a special favourite; likewise "Under the Red Robe,"
by Stanley Weyman.

Subject B was not nearly so popular with the girls as with the boys,
but the compositions on it were to a great extent free from the exaggerated tone and unreal sentiment which so much disfigured the boys'
work on the same subject.

I have no serious fault to find with the spelling, grammar, or handwriting of most of the candidates; many of them were awarded extra
marks for general neatness and attention to details, which, in the case
of the boys, was quite an exceptional occurrence.

From the foregoing remarks it must not be inferred that I am entirely satisfied with the compositions of the girls, taken as a whole. Such is very far from being the case; for, when I state that only about 17 per cent. obtained half marks, while about 38 per cent. were awarded less than quarter marks, it will be at once perceived what a large amount of room there is for improvement in respect to the writing of English Composition.

The questions on GRAMMAR and PARSING were not very well answered, but in working out the exercise in ANALYSIS, intelligence, care, and method were generally displayed, which, combined with a good knowledge of the subject, secured high marks for most of the candidates.

The answering in the MILTON was good, and gave evidence of careful preparation. In replying to Question 6 ("Quote the lines from *Lycidas* referring to St. Peter") a great many girls, instead of merely quoting the five lines referring to St. Peter, wrote out, in addition, the whole of St. Peter's speech to Lycidas—some twenty lines or so—thus wasting a large amount of valuable time. In explaining the marked words and passages in Question 8 some bad mistakes were made, such as, in the passage "He by Friar's lantern led," explaining "Friar's lantern" to mean "the altar lamp," "a star," "the reflection of the moon," and so forth. Then, again, the passage "to outwatch the Bear with thrice-great Hermes" drew forth some curious explanations, but nothing to compare with the ideas entertained by some of the boys as to its meaning. However, these cases were exceptional, and, on the whole, the questions on Milton were answered very satisfactorily.

The GRAY does not appear to have been studied as intelligently as the Milton, and the remarks I have made upon the boys' answering in it apply with nearly equal force to the girls. In very few instances was the prose paraphrase of the *Elegy* (Question 9) really well done, and the line "Their furrow oft the stubborn glebe has broke" (Question 10 (b)), gave rise to quite a crop of ingenious blunders, none, however, quite so absurdly fanciful as some of those committed by the boys in the same connexion. In "Stout Gloster stood aghast" (Question 10 (a)) the reference was in several instances said to be to the Duke of Gloucester afterwards Richard III., and in "Hauberk's twisted mail" (Question 10 (a)) "hauberk" was occasionally taken to be a proper name. The ten lines of the Bard's lamentation over his dead brother-bards (Question 11) were correctly quoted by the great majority of the candidates, boys as well as girls. This deserves especial notice, as no hint was supplied to "give them a start"; so that in answering this question something more than a mere effort of memory was involved.

MIDDLE GRADE.—SECOND PAPER.—BOYS.

Report of S. J. MACMULLEN, B.A.

The subjects were :—Selected Essays of Goldsmith; History of England and Ireland, 1603–1714 ; Outlines of English Literature from Chaucer to Milton, both inclusive ; Geography.

The candidates divide themselves by their answering into two classes, the strong and the weak, with a very wide interval between. The knowledge of the strong candidates is valuable; the knowledge of the weaker candidates, on the other hand, is so poor in quantity and quality, that it never could be of service to them or to anybody else.

In the work sent up there is not much, though there is some, evidence of teaching. Many of the candidates seem to have been pretty well left to themselves. Now, in the case of the strong candidates, boys of intellectual gift and working under educational influence in other studies, this did not matter much. But very many of the weak candidates would have answered much better, and therefore scored much higher, had they worked under steady, *competent* supervision.

The paper set tests only acquisition. The amount of knowledge to be acquired is, rightly, not very great; its chief value consists in the use a judicious teacher can make of it in forming the minds and enlarging the intellectual view of his pupils. That this course of study has been turned to account in this way there is not much evidence. Rather it would seem that the boys have been set to "get up" the statements in the text-books as far as possible word for word,—a process which, in the case of weak pupils, results in such hash as that presented in the following examples, taken from hundreds, some perhaps not so bad, some worse:—

(*a.*) "Bacon's Essays were chiefly on his visits to America and other exploits during his life."

(*b.*) "Some of them [the poets of Italy] got high places at court, such as Tully, Cicero, and Bourt—the great sculptor and painter."

(*c.*) "Hampden was a man who was put up to taking an action against his master for receiving a bribe."

(*d.*) [The leaders of the so-called Metaphysical School of English poetry] "were Homer, Virgil, Milton and Dante."

(*e.*) [The great Equatorial current of the Atlantic Ocean] "enters at the Atlantic, goes away round the coast and turns in at the bay of biscay, and discharges itself at the entrance of Germany until it gets out along the coast of Germany, and there it takes its direction."

(*f.*) [Franz-Joseph Land is] "noted for tobacco, currants and oranges."

It is gratifying to find that there is a distinct improvement in the mode of presenting the answers to the Examiner. It is now only the very weakest candidates that bite up their answers into fragments, and drop them on to the paper in any order. And that other bad habit —to which I referred last year—of hiding away answers, or parts of answers, in the blank leaves at the end of the answer-book, has all but disappeared.

MIDDLE GRADE.—SECOND PAPER.—GIRLS.

Report of S. J. MACMULLAN, M.A.

The subjects were :—Selected Essays of Goldsmith ; History of England and Ireland, 1603-1714 ; Outlines of English Literature from Chaucer to Milton, both inclusive ; Geography.

There is more symmetry in the work of the girls than in the work of the boys ; that is to say, the strongest candidates are not separated from the weakest by so wide an interval. The work, except in a very few cases, is not of first rate, or even of high, quality. '

There is distinct evidence of amazing industry and of careful supervision. But unfortunately the industry is often misapplied, as, e.g., when Goldsmith's estimate of Shaftesbury is learned off by heart—and then (here defective supervision comes in)—given in the examination as Goldsmith's estimate of Bolingbroke—or L'Estrange. Time and labour would be much better bestowed in getting at a distinct conception of these writers, even as they are expounded in the Essay, than in learning by rote the *ipsissima verba* of Goldsmith. While, therefore, the girls show marvellous industry and self-denial, their success in winning marks is not commensurate with the efforts (in themselves praiseworthy) of both pupils and teachers.

Another all-pervading weakness in these answers is—inaccuracy ; and inaccuracy means a low mark. Special pitfalls, set quite unintentionally, were—the inscriptions over the gates in the Gardens of Quasmé (*Pervia Virtuti; Facilis Descensus*). Then there was the spelling of Caribbean, Sweden (*Carrihean, Carribian, Sweeden—passim, Sweedon*) ; but the titles of Milton's prose works proved the most fruitful in blunders. The boys' papers also swarm with these same mistakes ; and boys and girls, in almost equal numbers, confound Buckingham with Marlborough, and Eugene with Rupert.

The boys are weak in Geography—it is the worst subject they bring up ; but the girls are quite surprisingly bad, considering their industry as shown in other parts of the course. They are like a certain schoolgirl at the beginning of the century, whose *Geography*, even when she was ending her school days, *left much to be desired*. But if the answering on the Geography questions is bad, the work on the map is worse. I do not know that I have ever seen greater ignorance displayed by examination-candidates. Many hundreds of marks have been lost in connection with the map. Here I note a curious circumstance. When a boy is unable to answer any of the map questions—when, in other words, he is unable to indicate one place out of ten places "set " on the map (Spain), he sends up his map *blank*. A girl, on the other hand, in the same case, usually prints with great care every one of the ten places mentioned in the examination paper on her blank map, etches-in the mountain chains—occupies, in short, a considerable portion of her examination-time—and does not earn a single mark. It is, I imagine, impossible to give any credit to a candidate who places, in however neat form, Santander on the site of Gibraltar, Barcelona at the mouth of the Tagus, Badajoz in the island of Majorca, the Sierra Nevada on the line of the Pyrenees, —and so of the rest.

On the whole, this work would be much more satisfactory if the candidates had mixed with their unquestioned industry and earnestness a little *reflection*—a little *judgment* ; had recognised and avoided in their studies the temptation to inaccuracy in thought and statement, and had not wholly neglected the geographical section of the course.

ENGLISH.

JUNIOR GRADE.—FIRST PAPER.—GIRLS.

Report of G. F. SAVAGE-ARMSTRONG, M.A., D.LIT.

I have the honour to report that, on the whole, the answering has shown, in my opinion, anxiety on the part of the candidates to do their very best; much zealous self-preparation; and a good deal of careful teaching. It is many years since I have taken part in any examination under the Intermediate Education Board, and I can freely say that I have observed on this occasion many signs of improvement in the quality of the work done by the candidates.

There is still evidence—and they are, perhaps, the worst features apparent—that the memory of the candidates is cultivated rather in excess of their understanding; that subjects, such as poetry, which are intended to be, and ought to be, a source of elevating enjoyment, are too much dinned into their minds as wearisome tasks; and that the teaching of English Composition is not efficient, its methods and principles being probably not properly comprehended.

There has been a very general facility in answering questions in poetry with passages learned off in parrot-like ignorance of their meaning; where the powers of thought and observation are called into play (as in parsing and analysis of sentences), there have been many failures; and, with rare exceptions, the compositions have been crude and uncultivated.

I have marked the compositions with leniency, because candidates so young cannot be expected to be furnished with many ideas or with much information, and without ideas and matter no really good essay can be produced. It was quite clear, too, that the faults of the compositions were not always due to any want of zeal or care on the part

which she has heard delivered from the pulpit of her house of worship.
She, accordingly, favours the Examiner with an ardent address, abounding in solemn exhortations and pathetic "ohs!" and "ahs!" This is the "Sermonic Style"—of the competitive examination variety. If the pupil has been really taught English essay-writing, she will not be likely to fall into such errors when she comes up to be examined.

In the formal exercise in punctuation many candidates showed accurate knowledge and skill; but in applying the rules of punctuation to their own compositions most of them went lamentably astray.

Some few candidates were so badly prepared in all branches of their work that it seemed almost a cruelty to subject them to an examination at all.

JUNIOR GRADE. —FIRST PAPER.

Report of W. P. COYNE, M.A., Rev. M. FOGARTY, D.D., and Rev. CORNELIUS MULCAHY.

We have pleasure in stating that the answering in the First Junior Grade paper in English was, considered all round, very satisfactory.

The Compositions were in a few cases excellent—in a few very poor indeed; while the greater number fulfilled all the conditions that could reasonably be looked for in the essays of Junior Grade boys. We take this average merit as a sign that this important and valuable branch of the examination is receiving more and more attention in the schools. There is, of course, still room for considerable progress. Thus some of the essays, and these evidently the work of fairly intelligent lads, showed a remarkable ignorance, on the part of the writers, of the proper limits of a sentence or of the laws of paragraph construction. In the matter of spelling, there is plenty of room for reform. Few papers, indeed, were free from gross blemishes in orthography. We frequently found glaring errors such as the following :—

> "*Mussels*" for muscles; "*spirits*," "*deride*";
> "And as a *hair* whom hounds and horns *pursue*";
> "'*Sweet*' said the *Ayle*, as she gave the gift," &c.

One Examiner, who took the trouble of estimating the number of variants of the title of Moore's "Lalla Rookh" which he found in his papers, arrived at a grand total of twenty five different, and all erroneous, spellings!

The passage given for correction, insertion of capitals, punctuation and quotation marks [Question 2] was, on the whole, very well done. This is the more commendable as the question was in the nature of a surprise one.

The passage given for analysis* was most indifferently handled. Out of every possible combination of errors we select the one which we found most frequent. In this "The service past" was described as the Principal Sentence : "Each honest rustic ran " as Subordinate, and the rest accordingly. The line given for parsing was Goldsmith's

> *Sure, scenes like these no troubles e'er annoy.*

> * "*The service past, around the pious sire,*
> *With steady zeal, each honest rustic ran.*"

The general answering on this was very poor. Quite 60 per cent. of
the answers were erroneous in some part, while such gross blunders as
making " scenes " nominative to the verb " annoy " and " troubles "
its direct object ; parsing " like " as a verb, and " annoy " as a noun
were regrettably frequent.

Wherever memory-work, pure and simple, was sufficient for the
answer, the questions were uniformly well done. This was markedly
so in the Quotations from the Authors. Here, however, we must
remark that while the " references " were, in almost every case, stated
correctly, and the passages located in their context, the "meaning" of the
passages was very often omitted, or an erroneous one attributed to them.

Great fluency in quotation was a general characteristic of the examinations. We should like to feel certain that mere memory is not
being cultivated at the expense of the higher intellectual powers—a
suspicion for which the general answering in the paper offers many
grounds. An error in quotation like the following—which was exceedingly common—shows that a great number of the students learnt
Moore's lines as a mere rhyme-jingle without any but the vaguest idea
of their import :

> " But see—alas !—the crystal bar
> Of Eden moves not—holier far
> That even this drop the brow must be
> That opes the gates of Heav'n for thee."

JUNIOR GRADE.—SECOND PAPER.—BOYS.

Report of Rev. F. F. CARMICHAEL, LL.D., JOHN D. COLCLOUGH, and
JOHN F. TAYLOR, B.A.

The questions from the *Spectator* were, on the whole, fairly answered,
though but in comparatively few instances could the reply be regarded
as complete. The quotation from the poet Antiphanes (Question 1a)
was seldom accurately given, and in their treatment of the second part
of the question, as in that of Question 3, the writers drew largely upon
their imagination ; no little skill and intelligence, however, were sometimes displayed in their answers, although, of course, no credit could be
given for such attempts.

The point of Question 3* was frequently missed, notwithstanding
that the word *humors* was italicised.

There was a decided improvement in the answers to the questions
in Irish History, indicating a more careful study of that subject.

With the exception of the replies to No. 15,* which were little more
than guess work, the answering in Geography was good.

The spelling, in a considerable number of instances, was largely open
to improvement, and there was also in such cases a want of neatness
and carefulness of writing to which the attention of teachers should be
especially called.

---

*1. (a.) Quote the passage from the poet Antiphanes about " deceased friends " with
which the *Spectator* expresses himself as being " very much pleased."
(b.) What three human passions, according to Addison, are extinguished by the consideration of Death ?
3. Through what human transmigrations does Jack Freelove, in his letter to the lady,
represent her monkey to have passed ?
15. How is soil made ? What work is performed by brooks and rivers ? What
becomes of rain ?

JUNIOR GRADE.—SECOND PAPER.—GIRLS.

Report of MARY A. LISTER, M.A.

The answering was, on the whole, satisfactory. There were several excellent candidates whose work showed good and intelligent teaching. Then there was a large number of fairly good candidates who failed to reach a high standard on account of insufficient preparation, and want of care in teaching.

The answering of the questions in the "Selections from the Spectator" was very good. Many candidates obtained full marks for one or more questions. That many ludicrous mistakes were made by ill prepared or dull students goes without saying.

The History questions were well answered by those who had a good memory. Others, even intelligent students, were often unable to answer them. My general impression is, that in teaching history the memory is cultivated often at the expense of the other faculties.

The Geography was the least satisfactory part of the paper. Most candidates tried to answer the questions, and many did so extremely well, but this was because they were easy. Very great ignorance and confusion of mind was displayed by many candidates. The teaching of geography appears to be unsatisfactory, indeed very defective on the whole. How could a child who had ever drawn a map of England say that Liverpool is one of the counties of Wales, and Manchester its chief town? And this is only one example of numerous similar mistakes, and is essentially a proof of bad teaching. I am aware that a reform in the teaching of geography is much needed, and the sooner the teachers make themselves acquainted with the best methods of instruction, the better for the children. Not one candidate answered correctly Question 15 : "How is soil made? What work is performed by brooks and rivers? What becomes of rain?" Many thought it referred to agriculture and commerce, not physical geography.

It is a pity that so many candidates (fully ten per cent.), are permitted to present themselves for examination, who are plainly quite unfit, and have not any chance of passing. To such children an examination, far from being a healthy stimulus, must be distinctly injurious.

Much more attention should be paid to style in answering by the majority of candidates.

The questions should be answered in order, one part should not be separated from another, clear and correct numbering is essential, a space should be left between each answer. Neglect of these details lowered the standard of several candidates. I must add that many papers were very creditable indeed, the answering clear, concise, and well arranged.

It might be worth while for teachers to remind their pupils that all appeals to an Examiner's "mercy," and entreaties to be allowed to pass, are so much time and paper wasted. The practice of making such appeals by ignorant students is too common, and cannot be too strongly condemned.

PREPARATORY GRADE.—FIRST PAPER.—BOYS.

Reports of JANE BARLOW, WILLIAM MACENNIS, M.A.; ARCHIBALD J. NICOLLS, LL.B.; and L. EDW. STEELE, M.A.

In general, the papers of the Preparatory Grade boys, and especially their Compositions, indicated the possession of a large measure of intelligence; but in too many cases it was painfully obvious that this natural ability had been neither judiciously developed nor wisely guided. In such cases the conviction was forced upon us that the teachers were concerned rather to secure that their pupils should "pass" the examination in some fashion, than that they should fairly understand the subjects of the English programme, and benefit intellectually by the year's study and instruction. This system of converting children into mere earners of results fees, to the detriment of their education, is promoted by many devices. We detected occasional traces of one device which can only be characterized as pernicious and demoralizing: before the candidate has even entered the examination hall his work of composition is done; he has been primed with an essay chosen, on speculation, from some author, and is supplied with a series of "introductions" from which to select, in order to adjust the memorized essay to the special requirements of the examination paper. The effect on the morale of the schools where this practice is pursued can be easily foreseen.

It is much to be feared that Grammar and Spelling do not receive the attention they require. Quite a large number of otherwise good papers are spoiled by such faults as even primary schools labour to correct. Provincialisms are of frequent occurrence, for instance: "They were *after* rowing a mile"; "Ships *does be* going to Liverpool"; "The captain would not *leave* them disembark." This use of "leave," meaning to permit, seems very prevalent; it is met with in papers studiously free from colloquial and objectionable phrases. As regards Spelling, no language can properly describe the vagaries in which these candidates indulged. A few quotations of the actual spellings must suffice: "*Iurn* (i.e. iron) is used for the *mountains* (mountings) of ships"; "*Iorn* is very useful for making *ornaments* such as *cross* and other household purposes"; *sord* (sord), *wowndid*, *sizsus* (scissors), *pinchers* (pincers), *britches*, *old* (hold). These examples reveal the style of speech and pronunciation which obtains in the schools from which the perpetrators hail.

Boys who have not the faintest conception of what parsing is, can score full marks in questions asking for the plurals of certain nouns; and many who cannot answer even these questions satisfactorily, can quote literally and voluminously from "The Deserted Village," and "The Prisoner of Chillon." Yet not a few who are thus familiar with the text, are absolutely ignorant of its meaning. The inference to be drawn from these facts is unmistakable.

In drawing attention to these shortcomings of candidates and to the unsatisfactory elements we thought apparent in the mode of preparation adopted by some of the teachers, we do not lose sight of the fact that the general level of merit was high, and that a considerable number of pupils displayed such marked proficiency as could only be attained in schools where the work of education was thoroughly carried out.

PREPARATORY GRADE.—FIRST PAPER.—GIRLS.

L. EDW. STEELE, M.A.

I have examined 712 answer-books on the First Paper (Composition, Grammar, and the Poetical Books), and beg to report that the answering as a whole was very satisfactory. The paper was not a difficult one, and consequently accuracy in the answers was looked for; some of the answer-books were really excellent, when the age of the candidates is considered. The orderliness observed in the arrangement of the answers, and the legibility of the writing, were worthy of praise, and reflect much credit on the instructors of the candidates.

English Composition.—The first subject given (" Any great disaster on sea or land which has interested you ") produced the best compositions ; the Kerry-Bog incident, and the Paris tragedy, supplying matter for many very good efforts. Although many did give evidence, yet a large number failed to show any, of an effort having been made to arrange some heads or points before the compositions were commenced. I noticed, for the first time, evident signs of some compositions having been carefully committed to memory ; for example, several, which were descriptions of shipwrecks, were merely ingenious paraphrases of ' The Wreck of the Hesperus.' As one would have expected, there was a marked absence of the dreadful school and street slang, which is so offensive in the boys' compositions. English composition is obviously a difficult subject to teach, but there remains very much to be done in the direction of supplying boys and girls with some simple plan to follow at an examination, such as would be suggested by having an introduction, a descriptive or argumentative portion, and a summary or peroration in every composition. The punctuation, as usual, was poor.

Grammar.—The punctuation exercise proved an excellent test. There were 35 possible corrections in the piece given, and not more than two or three candidates obtained full marks : some of the attempts were very bad, but a large number proved satisfactory. Notwithstanding the explicit directions, many insisted on altering the phraseology of the passage. The parsing was not good. In the first lines of the excerpt—

" Thus much the fathom-line was sent
From Chillon's snow-white battlement,"

a large number parsed " *was sent*," instead of what was indicated by the italicising.

Literary portion—The Deserted Village and Prisoner of Chillon.—The memory work was excellent ; nearly all the candidates gave the quotations most accurately, and as if they understood their meaning, there being very little of a mere phonetic, ill-spelt re-echoing of the words of the poems, which I have observed on previous occasions.

The least satisfactory answers were to those questions which demanded explanations. For example ; in *Quest.* 6, where an explanation of " *the sickly trade*" was required—("There the pale artist plies the *sickly trade*") quite a large number accepted the word *artist* as equivalent to *painter of pictures*, and ascribed the sickliness of his occupation to the poisonous nature of his paints! To *Quest.* 9 (on The Prisoner of Chillon), in the lines—

" And cheering from my dungeon's brink
Had brought me back to feel and think,"

the following answer was repeated over and over again ;—" *dungeon's brink* is the brink of death to which he had come in the dungeon." When the words merely require the simple explanation, that they refer to the little window of the prisoner's dungeon, this elaborate one is the more extraordinary. Again, in the same question—

" I had no hope my eyes to raise,
And clear them of their dreary mote,"

the following note was received on a great number of the papers: "mote — a particle of dust in the eye; dreary mote, the mote which caused the prisoner's eyes to drip dismal tears." These examples would suggest that the candidates had used some annotated edition of the poems which had been put into their hands without due consideration as to its suitability; a serious matter when marks are lost thereby, and one worth the attention of school authorities.

PREPARATORY GRADE.—SECOND PAPER.—BOYS.

Report of Rev. DANIEL COGHLAN, D.D., and EILEEN KINGSTON, B.A.

The questions were, on the whole, fairly well answered: the candidates seem to have prepared their work well, and the defects to which we shall have to allude are, we are sure, mainly due to the intellectual immaturity of youth, and not to defective training.

The answering on the Spectator was, on the average, good. But it was obvious, in some cases, that the memory only had been exercised, and that the meaning of the author had not been apprehended; and consequently the answering was sometimes defective, where the questions required a knowledge of the subject matter of the Essays.

The questions in English History were, generally speaking, fairly well answered. But the answering in Irish History was not so generally satisfactory; which would seem to point to the disagreeable fact that the careful teaching of Irish History is not so general amongst us, as of English History.

In Geography, Ireland seems to have been well studied; but the answering in general Geography was, in many cases, inaccurate and defective.

PREPARATORY GRADE.—SECOND PAPER.—GIRLS.

Report of WILLIAM GRAHAM, M.A.

The answering of the Girls in the Preparatory Grade was, on the whole, fairly good, though the marking was not quite so high as on the last occasion when I examined this Grade. I do not, however, think the latter result was due to their being less well prepared, but merely to the fact that the questions in English Literature this year were possibly a shade harder than on the previous occasion.

COMMERCIAL ENGLISH.

SENIOR GRADE.—BOYS AND GIRLS.

Report of WILLIAM GRAHAM, M.A.

In the Senior Grade, Commercial English, the number of boys who presented themselves for examination was not great; but the average answering was very good, while the highest was excellent, two attaining over 75 per cent. The intelligence shown in deciphering the copying manuscript left something to be desired, being, as it was, a shade less than that shown by the same grade of students when last examined by me. It should, however, be added that the exercise laid before them this year, being on a financial subject, had in it an unusual number of technical terms requiring for their comprehension special knowledge as well as general intelligence, so that I do not think that, on the whole, there has been any falling off in the standard of attainment in this branch.

Much the same may be said of the girls' answering as of the boys in the Senior Commercial English. The answering, indeed, was not of quite so high a level, and the best was not so good as in the case of the boys; but the chief difference between them, to the advantage of the latter, came from the fact that the girls made guesses much wider of the mark in their rendering of the copying manuscript. As stated with regard to the boys' paper, this was on a financial subject, with which presumably girls without special reading are less acquainted than boys.

MIDDLE GRADE.

In the Middle Grade, Commercial English, the answering presented a good steady average, with very few failures, in a total of sixty six candidates. In the case of the best student the answering reached the exceptionally high score of 375 out of 400. The answering of the girls was a shade inferior, but only a shade. As in the case of the Senior Grade, the subject of the copying manuscript was financial, with the result that while the handwriting was generally good, the knowledge required for interpretation of the manuscript was a little wanting.

JUNIOR GRADE.—BOYS and GIRLS.

Report of JOHN PARR, D.LITT.

I examined in Commercial English, Junior Grade, the answers of 310 boys and 30 girls. Though they were often meagre and insufficient, and sometimes wildly wrong, they seem to mark an advance since 1894 when I examined similar papers, in respect of neatness, information, capacity to take a hint, and general intelligence. Here Geography has—and, in my opinion, very properly—more value than History, and it was better prepared; the weakest part of the work was the copying manuscript, which too often betrayed a sadly defective vocabulary, and a surprising ignorance of current phrases and expressions.

PRÉCIS WRITING.

SENIOR AND MIDDLE GRADES.—BOYS AND GIRLS.

Report of ARCHIBALD J. NICOLLS, LL.B.

Many of the Précis papers examined by me this year for the Commissioners of Intermediate Education were very satisfactory. This applies equally to the work of Senior Grade and Middle Grade pupils.

Several Middle Grade candidates showed but very slight knowledge of the correct method of work. They lacked power of condensation, and failed to collect the salient points in the file of correspondence put before them.

G 3

In my opinion the heads of schools undervalue Précis as a subject of study. I call special attention to this, because the number of pupils presenting for the examination bore no fair proportion to the number of students in either grade.

This is remarkable, and to be regretted : for proficiency in Précis is essential, in many cases, to the advancement of those who devote themselves to commerce or to any branch of the Civil Service.

FRENCH.

Senior Grade.—Boys.

Report of Albert M. Selss, LL.D.

In looking over the 278 Boys' Senior Grade answer books, submitted to me for examination, I was agreeably surprised by the correct rendering of most of the French passages set for translation into English. There were few, if any, failures in this part of the answering. The case was different in attempts at French composition, which were less successful, thus corroborating the common observation that a student may be able to understand whole pages of French, and to translate them fairly into English, and yet not know how to write or say one dozen words of his own in accurate grammatical French.

A new and interesting feature of the recent examination is the attempt at describing the sound of French words by means of English, and the introduction of questions bearing on the pronunciation. A successful advance in this direction is most desirable, because it would meet a standing reproach made to the system of Intermediate Examinations, viz., that they rely exclusively on *written* proofs of knowledge, and consequently ignore the *audible element* in Modern Languages. I have watched the result of the new experiment in the case before me, and am happy to say that means the employed, though not a perfect substitute for *vivâ voce* examination, yet seemed to me to involve a fair approach to oral tests, and that, therefore, such questions on pronunciation ought to be continued, and should form a permanent feature of all French examinations in the future.

About one-tenth of the candidates had omitted the questions relating to this subject ; about three-fifths had given imperfect answers, and the other three-tenths had battled successfully with the questions asked. It would be unfair to set down the imperfections to sheer ignorance.

The questions set on the matter of the text-books were all readily taken in hand, and answered with spirit, even if they led, here and there, to mistakes. Among these questions I especially include those on European history and literature. There is nothing that affords so good a test of general knowledge, and nothing that relieves so agreeably and so usefully the dryness of merely linguistic tests, as this class of questions.

SENIOR GRADE—GIRLS.

Report of PAUL BARBIER.

The pronunciation of the combinations of the letters *ll*, *rr*, in the words *fille*, *ville*, *fourrai*, and *courrai*—Question 1—was imperfectly represented. The Grammar questions were, on the whole, creditably answered. Creditable as they were, they do not come up to the standard of accuracy of the Middle Grade. The weakest points were—(1) the rendering of the sentences illustrating the use of the subjunctive mood; question 4. (Most of the candidates laid the rules down correctly, and yet were unable to apply the rules)—(2) the answering as to the rules on the agreement of past participles of reflexive verbs. The cases of the oblique personal pronouns governed by *faire* in front of an infinitive, were generally badly explained. The prose composition was much below the standard of that of the Middle Grade. Though the vocabulary was fair, the syntactical order of words, and the use of past tenses, imperfect and perfect, were indeed weak. The candidates were ill prepared in this important part of French syntax. Notwithstanding my lenient attitude on this question, very few of the candidates obtained a third of the marks. The translations of prepared work were excellent; some were remarkable for their literary finish; so were the quotations from the fable—a feature which indicates the candidates had been well trained and taught in this particular section of the paper. The translations at sight were satisfactory: they, however, revealed a poverty of vocabulary,—words, as *brin*, *charbonneret*, *mouchoir*, *mintou*, *poiguet*, *hangars*, *herse*, *bambou*, etc., were given extraordinary meanings. Translating extracts from various writers would rectify this weak feature.

MIDDLE GRADE—BOYS.

Report of PAUL BARBIER.

The candidates wrote a fair representation of the pronunciation of the typical French words, *femme*, *cinq*, *nationaux*; the combinations of the letters *ll*, *gn*, in the words *briller*, *agneau*, were very imperfectly shown. *Gn* is fairly heard in *ni* of the English word *pinion*, and *ller* in the word *yea*. The answers to the Grammar questions were good, although somewhat uneven. The answers to the Question 3 on composing sentences to illustrate *autral*, *chacun*, *ni l'un*, *ni l'autre*, &c.; those to the Question 5 on translating into French *will there have been any*, *they would have to run*, *I would not have sung*, were poor. Coupling the translations of these sentences with that of *if she would play of the* prose composition, I came to the conclusion that the candidates were not able to discriminate the functions of *would*, *will*, &c., as auxiliaries from *would*, *will*, &c., as independent verbs. The colloquial sentences were good indeed. The prose composition was uniformly well done. Many candidates exhibited a French living ring that induces me to think that their proficiency is not only due to book training, but greatly to their having had colloquial practice. The manner in which the candidates translated the past tenses in this section and in the prose section was admirable; the only weak point was the rendering of the past tense of *How long were you in this school?*—Question 7 (a). I have not

examined a piece of prose composition for years that has given me more
satisfaction and shown so much progress in the teaching of French in
Ireland. The translations of prepared passages were good; that, however, of some of the idiomatic sentences partook of the character of
guessing work. The explanations of sentences of (*b*), question 8—*je ne
demande pas mon plus, il n'y a pas de quoi*, &c.—were poor, which must be
ascribed to these sentences being overlooked in reading the set books.
The scanning of French verse was a perfect blank. It is impossible to
understand fully the beauty of French verse if the students be not taught
the syllabic division of words. The annexe paper (II) translations, in
marked contrast with the other sections of the paper, were very unsatisfactory. The very first word, *qui*, misled many into mere guessing
work. A more rigorous parsing of French words, somewhat on the
lines of the rigorous method of parsing Latin, would enable candidates
to understand fully the various syntactical functions of *qui*.

MIDDLE GRADE.—GIRLS.

Report of PAUL BARBIER.

The remarks and observations on the answers sent in by the boys
are also applicable to the work sent in by the girls.

The girls answered the question on pronunciation with more
accuracy than the boys.

Both boys and girls neglected the importance attaching to the right
use of signs *aigu*, and grave in the reinforcement of the vowel E.
Marks are lost by this carelessness.

JUNIOR GRADE.—BOYS.

Report of E. JAVAL, V. OGER, and F. SPENCER, M.A.

Notwithstanding a sprinkling of unprepared candidates, some of
whom did not attempt a single question, the results of this year's
examination show undeniable progress in almost every part of the work.

Too many candidates not only wrote their answers without any reference to the number of the questions, but scattered fragments of a
single answer over several pages of their answer books. Nothing could
excuse the slovenly character of some of the papers thus presented, and
teachers should obviate its recurrence by training the candidates to
write their answers in a careful and orderly manner.

Many mistakes are still found in English grammar and orthography,
not a few of which render unintelligible the sentences in which they
occur. The standard in this respect is, however, gradually improving.

With regard to the details of the paper, the following points deserve
special notice.

(1.) The answers to question 1 (on accents and sounds) were generally
very unsatisfactory, and in most cases the "accents" were more correctly done than the "sounds." It was thus evident that a large proportion of candidates had not the most elementary notion of French
pronunciation. Some, indeed, failed altogether to understand the pur-

port of the question, and contented themselves with translating into English the sentences designed as a test in pronunciation.

(2.) In each there was very general weakness, and, in spite of the plain and straightforward nature of the question, confusion between two distinct verbs and between different tenses of the same verb was very common.

(3.) Question 5 (on adverbs and adverbial phrases) was seldom answered intelligently or correctly.

(4.) The Composition showed a decided advance on the work of previous years, and was more generally attempted than usual, a fair proportion of papers being exceedingly creditable. In the continuous passage gross blunders were often so numerous as to render the whole of no practical value. Exceedingly few candidates were able to translate the phrases : "take a letter to the post and get it registered ; " and : " after washing our hands and faces."

(5.) The "prepared" translation from French into English was, on the whole, fairly done, but seldom really well ; and the instructions given in the paper were often neglected. The translation by many candidates of detached sentences from the prescribed work showed conclusively that preparation of the worst mechanical type is still far from rare.

(6.) Both passages for translation at sight were very well rendered by many candidates, but many more entirely failed to grasp even their general sense, and a version intelligently begun often degenerated into unintelligible jargon.

Reviewing the work as a whole, and comparing it with that of previous years, we regard it as satisfactory and decidedly hopeful.

JUNIOR GRADE.—GIRLS.

Report of W. F. BUTLER, M.A.

The answers of the candidates for Junior Grade, Girls, French, in 1897, have been marked, on the whole, by a very great uniformity.

The standard attained cannot, except in a very few cases, be called high, the answers of the vast majority being on a dead level, by no means good, but quite sufficient for a pass.

In Grammar, both as tested by the actual Grammar questions, and by the Composition, a great tendency is to be observed to get up exceptions and irregularities rather than what may be called a working knowledge of the language.

The same tendency is to be noted in the Composition, where simple colloquial phrases seemed to present far greater difficulties than questions involving grammatical peculiarities.

As regards the prescribed text-books many candidates had evidently only made up one of the authors required.

There is no special remark to be made on the unprescribed pieces except that many candidates were quite unacquainted with the word " Char."

PREPARATORY GRADE.—BOYS.

Report of JOHN W. BACON, M.A., and EDMOND J. M'WEENEY, M.A.

In comparison with last year's results we find that the standard of answering is on the whole well maintained. Considering the youth of the candidates, their knowledge of French Grammar is highly satisfac.

tory. With regard to French Composition we find the colloquial phrases well translated by a large majority of the candidates, whereas a great number failed at the continuous passage. The reverse was the case with the translation from French into English, for the continuous passage was almost always accurately rendered, whereas candidates for the most part failed to grasp the meaning of the isolated phrases taken from the prescribed author. In the "translation at sight" a noticeable feature was the lack of practice exhibited by candidates in dealing with this form of exercise, and we think it would be well if teachers were more frequently to direct the attention of pupils to passages and authors outside the prescribed course.

PREPARATORY GRADE.—GIRLS.

Report of F. J. AMOURE.

The paper has been done very creditably on the whole. Among the unavoidable failures, there is still a number of candidates, fifty at least, that must have known or should have been told that they had not the slightest chance of obtaining a pass. The answers to the grammatical questions show good grounding and promise well for the future. The composition, as usual, is the hardest test, the continuous piece especially proving unmanageable to many for want of an adequate vocabulary; on the other hand nearly every paper shows some knowledge of elementary French idioms. The translation from the set book "Mon Famille" is the least satisfactory part of the whole paper. The consecutive passage is well done, but the detached sentences have produced many failures. The inference is obvious: pupils are apt to commit a story to memory and manage well enough when the context helps them, but they fare badly with the isolated words and phrases, to which they have neglected to pay sufficient attention. Too many candidates failed to understand the meaning of "word for word" and of "parallel column," and lost marks in consequence. A little practice beforehand would easily set that matter right. I must not conclude without congratulating the candidates on the methodical manner in which the different parts of the paper have been treated. With very few exceptions, every question has been answered in due order and fully before the next one was attempted.

COMMERCIAL FRENCH.

JUNIOR, MIDDLE, AND SENIOR GRADES.—BOYS AND GIRLS.

Report of ELPHEGE JANAU.

Middle Grade. Out of 84 boys there are 35 failures, and out of 36 girls 31 failures—only 3 girls obtaining honours.

In this grade also the handwriting left very much to be desired, especially in the case of the girls; whilst the spelling showed in many cases ignorance of every day words such as coffee, bales, coarse, weight, business.

The translations from French into English were fair, but some candidates must have been strangely prepared who could mistake *tare* for the name of an author.

In the sentences to turn into French the phrase "account receipted" was not translated correctly by any candidate. From the translation of these and of the longer pieces of composition it was evident that in many cases phrases had been learnt and were used irrespective of their meaning.

Most candidates in this grade will have to work very hard to pass the superior grade.

Junior Grade.—The candidates for the Junior Grade were much better prepared than those for the higher grades.

Both pieces of translation from French into English were satisfactory, and showed that the candidates had learnt a large number of words. The detached sentences and phrases to turn into English were not so well done.

The Composition was poor, in many cases very poor indeed. Two many candidates paid no regard to the most elementary rules of grammar, and frequently the verb was in the first person with a subject in the second. It would be better to limit such candidates to the general paper, and employ in the study of the ordinary language the time now given to Commercial French.

Still, on the whole, the examination proved that conscientious work had been done by both teachers and pupils. If the more successful candidates go on studying earnestly they ought to produce very good work in the higher grades.

GERMAN.

SENIOR, MIDDLE, JUNIOR, PREPARATORY GRADES.
BOYS AND GIRLS.

Report of V. STEINBERGER, M.A.

General Remarks.

1. The poor answering of the questions on pronunciation reveals a very weak spot in the teaching of a foreign language, and reduces such teaching almost to a farce. The very word "language" reminds us that the *lingua* should play the essential part in this branch of knowledge. Whilst abstract grammar must occupy an important place, yet the principal aim of the instruction in Modern Languages ought to be the practical use of them for speaking. There are, no doubt, difficulties in the way, especially when large classes are to be taught; but if the teacher were to read, at the beginning of each lesson, aloud and distinctly, a few sentences of foreign text, and have them re-read aloud, and ... ... by the pupils, good results would be obtained in

a short time, and the practical side of the teaching advanced considerably. The pupil will, by degrees, get his organs adapted, and his ears accustomed to the strange sounds, and acquire a certain confidence in speaking the foreign tongue. It is the want of sufficient practice in pronounciation which deters the young student from making a practical use of what he has acquired by memory. Immense harm, moreover, is done by not early accustoming the pupils to pronounce correctly, because they will of necessity create a pronounciation of their own which they find later on very difficult to unlearn.

2. It has become a practice with a great many candidates to give two or three answers to one question. Some of those answers are right, others are wrong. This style of answering is to be deprecated. No credit can be given to such guess-work.

3. Contrary to my former experience, I found that the boys' answering was better, and showed a more thorough knowledge, than that of the girls; most of the latter go astray in the composition. Regular composition work done very carefully, and repeated from time to time, will remedy this defect.

SENIOR GRADE.

The answering in this grade has been good, with the exception of the Grammar questions two, three, and four :—

2. Turn, in German, the following passage in the direct speech (*oratio recta*) into the indirect speech (*oratio obliqua*) :—

Der Fortwähler antwortis: „Sie haben mir mitgeteilt Freiheit Blik und mich zu bringen sehen Verband gewesen; und Sie gehen vor, sie zu sehen, Sie sie muß beruhigtbachi haben?"

3. Give the German for : to be content with it ; to be jealous of them ; to be proud of them ; to be angry with him ; we remembered him ; he was a friend of ours ; be of good cheer !

4. Remark the strong accent, and translate : Du hast ihn wohl geführt; du hast ihn mehr gesehen; es hat ihn doch wohl gesehen; du hast ihn doch wohl ihm gesehen.

Question four was only guessed at by the majority of candidates.
The composition was done fairly well. The verb "put" in the sentence, "One of them put a letter into his hands," was translated properly by only a few. A great many used the verb „stellen" An explanation of the difference of the verbs: stellen, legen, legen will facilitate the translation of the English verb "to put."
Prescribed books were well prepared, and the rendering of the translation at sight gave evidence that the candidates possessed a good vocabulary.

MIDDLE GRADE.

The impression left, after reading the papers of all the grades, was that the candidates of this grade answered best. The boys' answering was especially good. The answers, however, given to grammar questions three and six showed weakness, especially the conjugation of the reflective verbs, „sich verfallen," and the imperfective subjunctive of „retten" and „bringen." In question six few could state the difference between fügen (conjugated with haben), folgen (with sein), befolgen, verfolgen, and erfolgen.

The detached sentences for translation were rendered in most cases admirably. In the continuous piece of composition, however, some candidates were not able to apply the rules of German construction which they had rightly applied in the detached sentences. This fault points to a want of practice in continuous composition.

The translation of the word „Schattenwert" puzzled many, and not a few showed their ingenuity by rendering it by "joy of having a shadow." The translation at sight was inferior to the rest of the work.

JUNIOR GRADE.

There was very incorrect and poor answering given to the first, fourth, and fifth grammar questions:—

1. Decline in both numbers (a) with the definite, and (b) with infinite article: der junge Deutsche; das wilde Gemüth; die harte Prüfung.

4. State the third person plural of the indicative pluperfect, of the first future, and of the second future, of: gefangen worden, sich haben, zu schreiben.

5. Enumerate those German consonants (single and compound) that are pronounced differently from the corresponding English ones.

Not unfrequently adjectives were modified when declined in the plural. The declension of the substantive „der Deutsche" offered difficulties. The conjugation of a passive and of a reflective verb seemed novelty to a great many, and only a few could even attempt question five.

Most candidates translated the English into German badly, because they had not sufficient practice in the rules of German construction; whilst, apparently, showing their knowledge of these rules in one sentence, they forgot, or were unable to apply them in the next.

The prepared translation was fair; the translation at sight middling.

PREPARATORY GRADE

The answering in this grade, considering the age of the candidates, was promising. With the exception of the first question in grammar, referring to pronunciation—"State those German vowel sounds which do not exist in English "—all the grammar questions were fairly answered.

Want of a sufficient vocabulary prevented most from writing a letter composition. The rendering of the prepared passages was, in general, good, and showed careful preparation. The translation at sight, however, was poor.

COMMERCIAL GERMAN.

The number of those who presented themselves for Commercial German is less than in former years, but the quality of the answering has improved. About half of the candidates translated very creditably the English commercial expressions and letters into German.

ITALIAN.

ALL GRADES.—BOYS AND GIRLS.

Report of Tutor Binns.

A general improvement in all grades was the most remarkable feature of nearly all the papers, when compared with those which I examined in 1885, 1886, 1890, and 1891. The evil, commonly called "cramming" was conspicuous by its absence; and quite nine tenths of the papers gave abundant proof that the real preparation for the examination was made from day to day throughout the term of study. Undoubted evidence of this was given, particularly by the Composition, which I consider the most important part, as it is the best test of the knowledge of a modern language.

It has been also very pleasing to remark that the candidates have attempted to answer (with the single exception mentioned below) all the questions of each Examination Paper.

The only question that was too often left unanswered was that placed on the paper to test the candidates' knowledge of Italian pronunciation. This question, No. 6 in each grade,* was simple enough; and yet hardly twenty per cent. of the candidates even attempted to answer it. This silence shows that such want of knowledge is to be attributed to the remissness of teachers rather than to the carelessness of students. The importance of orthoepy in the study of a modern language is too patent to need recommendation.

The Grammar was good in almost all the Papers of every Grade; and the syntactical rules were well illustrated, except in the case of some candidates of the Preparatory Grade.

The text-books had been thoroughly and uniformly well studied, their translation showing pretty nearly equal merit. Yet the candidates' knowledge of cognate subjects, closely allied to the subject matter of the text-books, proved very deficient in many cases. Questions on the history or literature of Italy were not often answered correctly, or were left unanswered.

In the Preparatory Grade the spelling of English words was frequently faulty—in two Papers there were more English words misspelt than Italian ones.

The Commercial Papers were, with a single exception, all well answered; although the candidates showed a poor acquaintance with technical words and phrases used in commerce. Students and their teachers should understand that it is not sufficient to answer in good Italian, but that it is necessary to know the language used by Italians in business.

---

* Senior Grade.—Explain how the soft sound of the letters "c" and "g" before the vowels "e" and "i" may be hardened, and how the hard sound of "c" and "g" before the vowels "a," "o," "u," may be softened.

Middle Grade.—Explain how, and in what case the Italian pronunciation of "gn" differs from the English, and give Italian sentences, each one of them containing one of the following words:—*argue, legno, ogni, ignorante,* and *ignudo.*

Junior Grade.—State whether any modification takes place in the pronunciation of Italian vowels when they are followed by "l," "m," or "n."

Preparatory Grade.—By what vowel is the sound of "gl" modified in Italian? State in which of the following Italian words the sound of "gl" is different from the sound of "gl" in English:—*gloria, giglio, globo, meglio, gleba,* and *egli.*

If all the candidates who take up Latin were acquainted with the fact that they could learn Italian as an additional subject with very little trouble and labour, they would doubly profit from the practical usefulness of their study.

I regret to say that too many Answer Books were filled with answers out of their numerical order; some students even going so far in slovenliness as to write a portion of an answer in one page and the remainder several pages after. Students should appreciate, far more than they seem to do, the importance of following in their answers the numerical order of the examination questions.

SPANISH.

ALL GRADES.—BOYS AND GIRLS.

Report of Rev. THOMAS WHEELER.

The few candidates who presented themselves for examination in Spanish in the Senior Grade gave proof of a very careful preparation of the authors, and a very accurate knowledge of the Grammar. The Compositions were good, showing in some cases a mastery of idiom quite remarkable.

The Junior Grade Papers also showed a fair knowledge of the Grammar, but some of the papers were rather carelessly compiled. It is to be regretted that the study of this rich and useful language is not more generally cultivated; and that both teachers and students do not yet seem to appreciate the advantages, literary and educational, which may be derived from the knowledge and study of it.

CELTIC.

PREPARATORY GRADE.—BOYS.

Report of DOUGLAS HYDE, LL.D.

The answering in the Preparatory Grade was rather weak. There was manifested a good deal of inattention to the questions set. Thus, when asked to write out the " synthetic " and " analytic " forms of the préfect of *tбim*, numbers of students wrote out the synthetic and analytic forms of *táim* itself. The translation from the Irish text set was generally good and intelligent, but a large proportion of students either came to grief over, or did not attempt, the unseen passage.

It was manifest from the answering and from the inability displayed to translate into Irish certain ordinary phrases, that next to none of the candidates had any acquaintance at all with it as a spoken language, but had studied it like other foreign languages only through the medium of text-books.

There was a distressing inability to distinguish between the use of *tá* and *is*, which might perhaps be overcome by impressing upon the memory two or three types of sentences constructed with each word.

Several of the students used a particular apparently self-invented script for the letter *a*, which they formed something like an u, with a stroke under it. It is to be hoped that they will either learn how to make a correct Irish *a*, or else use a Roman one. The Irish *s*, also, was sometimes formed carelessly like a *p*. The slightest attention would rectify this.

JUNIOR GRADE.

There was a great advance in the knowledge of Irish displayed in this grade, in comparison with that of the Preparatory students, and this was particularly the case with regard to the translation from sight. There was not nearly so much inattention to the questions asked, but even here a great number of the students when declining *an tridhely* mistook the Irish *t* for an *r*.

There was the same evidence as in the Preparatory Grade, that scarcely any of the students were acquainted with the Irish language as a spoken form of speech, numbers of them not being able to translate so ordinary a phrase as "How do you do."

In answering the questions out of the Irish Phrase Book many of the students unconsciously betrayed the fact that they must have got their answers by heart, as was evidenced by their sometimes giving what would have been an answer to a sentence not asked, as an answer to one that was. Thus, when a line from the Phrase Book was given, the translation of which would be "it divides the globe exactly in two," and when the student construes it as "they compelled a certain youth who passed to carry his cross," the inference is obvious, or when the Irish of "one dog alone will set all the dogs of the village barking" is translated, "he who meddles with strife is like one catching a dog by the ears," the principle upon which the student did his preparation becomes evident.

There was a good deal of the same inability to distinguish between the use of *is* and *tá* that marked the Preparatory Grade, and scores of students wrote such sentences as *tá fear maith é*, or *is bó ann seo bpáirc*.

MIDDLE GRADE.

There was a well-maintained advance in the sixty or seventy students who presented themselves in the Middle Grade, and there was a marked improvement in Irish composition. Here, too, there was evidence, but of a different sort, of the lack of acquaintance with Irish as a vernacular language. In this case it was evidenced by the curious obsolete words and forms employed by the students in place of the ordinary colloquial ones, as *ah-aithle* "after," *sith* a leap, *ibh* "drink," *tomaill* "eat," *ris* for *leis*, *ro* for *do*, etc. The tendency to Anglicise which has worked such havoc with native names during the last hundred years was in evidence here too, as when a student irreverently wrote of Mileadh [called Milesius in Latin, the ancestor of the Milesians] as Milly, and when several of them wrote *loch* for loch or lough.

The translation of the unseen passage was generally fair, but in answering the grammar questions there was a sad misplacement of dots and omission of accents.

SENIOR GRADE.

There were only twenty who presented themselves for examination in this Grade, and the answering in a rather difficult course was in every way creditable and good.

PREPARATORY GRADE.—GIRLS.

The girls who presented themselves in Celtic in this Grade were not numerous, nor is there any particular remark to be made about their answering, which was uniformly fair.

JUNIOR GRADE.—GIRLS.

The answering of the girls in this Grade was also of a creditable character. Their failings were of the same nature as those of the boys, but their papers were, perhaps, distinguished by greater neatness.

MIDDLE GRADE.—GIRLS.

Only two girls presented themselves in this Grade, and both did well.

DOMESTIC ECONOMY.
GIRLS ONLY.

SENIOR GRADE.

Report of M. J. DARRINGTON WARD, M.A.

The answering of the Senior Candidates is, in the main, very creditable. Very few cases of failure occurred, and high marks were gained by the majority of the candidates. A considerable amount of practical domestic knowledge was exhibited, while the scientific facts connected with the subject have been, on the whole, carefully acquired. There is, however, still a lingering attempt, here and there, to guess at the meaning of questions on which the candidate has no real information, and sometimes the flood-gates are opened widely to let in page after page of irrelevant matter, or superfluous detail, which the wording of the question does not warrant. Teachers should give their pupils more extensive and prolonged practice in the art of answering questions in writing, so as to aim at a pithy, well ordered style, and to avoid redundancy or reiteration. Neglect to observe the precise wording of the question on *life insurance* was a matter of common occurrence, and it led, of course, to loss of marks in this particular case. The question asked for fundamental principles, not for the common details of life insurance, which are familiar to most educated young people without special study. The first question on the paper* was also misunderstood by many. Criticism of an author's statement does not necessarily suggest the supply of multitudinous details of collateral information. In their anxiety to display to the Examiner their stores of knowledge on sanitary matters, many girls lost sight of the main point of this question, which was to show that personal habit and personal information can do much to check disease and combat common ailments. Elaborate rules for avoiding "cold," and ventilating or draining a house, were not required, nor indeed expected, in the answer to this particular question.

The papers are much more free from errors in spelling and eccentricity of handwriting than those which I examined some years ago in the same grade.

* 1. "A very large number of the diseases or disorders to which the human body is subject are most certainly due to circumstances that can be removed or avoided." Criticise this statement.

MIDDLE GRADE.

Report of FANNIE GALLAHER.

What struck me most in examining the Middle Grade answer-books in Domestic Economy this year, was the success of a large majority of the candidates in failing to know more. It seemed to me that many of them had achieved ignorance under great strain, for one cannot think it was easy for them to pin their faith to "oxtails" as "a sort of shell-fish," or to be ready to contrast them as "weekly stories" with leguminous plants. If I were to cast blame for this state of affairs in any direction I should be tempted to take aim at the mothers and deputy-mothers whose business it is not to possess considerable daughters with so little knowledge of the simplest ways of domestic life. Some, I fear, have a habit of sending the rawest of raw material to "Intermediate" teachers, and of expecting them to weave it, within a year or two, into serviceable stuff. But if the raw material is poor what can the teacher do in that length of time, and with so many other claims pressing? Presumably, Middle Grade candidates have, at least, a Junior Grade light as a foundation, and the juniors may be supposed to start their examination course with the "abc" of every subject at their command. But there's where the pity of it is! The supposition is fallacious. Many of the future candidates reach the hands of the teacher full sure that "digestion" is a naughty word, that the stomach is in the heart, that we swallow through our windpipe, and that the veins of the lungs carry the food into the right "oracle" where it is acted upon by the "saliva." There are others who declare emphatically, even at the end of their year's training, that stewing and cooking are two totally different processes, and that 6 lbs. of meat per day is the very least you should give any man.

In pity I stand on the side of the teachers this time, and if I might make a suggestion it would be to the effect that some authoritative action should, in the development of educational events, be taken whereby it would be impossible for such raw material to exist at the age of fifteen. Let instruction in the rudiments of domestic economy begin compulsorily at a very early age, and let the future rulers of households be made acquainted with, and interested in the initial laws of their domain before they come to think seriously of junior, or even preliminary, examinations. The *inside* part of us individually is the fate of our food; the *outside* part of us individually is the management of our home; let the future women of nations be set to know something of both of these and of their kindred subjects, as soon as they leave off plaiting straws in the kindergarten, and while they are girding themselves to encounter the trials of geometry, Latin grammar, political geography, and still more abstract studies.

JUNIOR GRADE.

Report of FANNIE GALLAHER and M. J. BARRINGTON WARD, M.A.

The answers of the Juniors in Domestic Economy this year impressed us with the belief that both matter and style might have been easily improved at the cost of a little more attention and earnestness on the part of teacher and pupil. The subject, as a whole, appeared to be treated too superficially, and very rarely was any anxiety to succeed visible. We found that questions depending on the information gained from the text-books were, in many cases, accurately answered, although seldom fully; but, where a practical knowledge of domestic processes was necessary, only a few of the candidates were qualified to give an opinion. Fewer still seemed to be conversant with the requirements of written examinations, and, therefore, we would venture to suggest that their teachers should pay more attention to instruction in the art of answering simple questions in writing. Some of the handwriting and spelling were ingeniously bad, but, as a rule, they might have been worse, and were worse not so very long ago. A tendency to trifle with the subject induced a good many candidates to answer apparently by the light of nature, without any definite preparation; while others, endowed with good memories, had acquired the exact wording of the text books by heart. The habit—so common with the seniors—of introducing much extraneous or superfluous matter around and about the simplest answer, seemed almost unknown among the juniors, whose papers were, in many instances, abnormally short as a consequence. There were several cases where the examination time was spun out by piteous appeals to the clemency of the examiners, poetic addresses, and irrelevant illustrations, all "bad form," to say the least of them.

PLANE TRIGONOMETRY.

SENIOR GRADE.—BOYS AND GIRLS.

Report of PATRICK KELLY.

The answering of the Senior Grade boys in Trigonometry was, on the whole, good, and in very many instances, of exceptional merit. The ordinary formulae of reduction and transformation were remembered with accuracy and applied with intelligence. The solutions were in many cases of singular neatness and originality.

It was a source of great pleasure to the examiner to find the same question solved in a variety of ways. The majority of the candidates had evidently been taught to think for themselves. There was no prevalent weakness in the answering to which it is necessary to direct attention.

The answering of the Senior Grade girls, though satisfactory, did not reach an equally high standard. It was obvious that the greater number of them had seriously applied themselves to the subject and, while the general level of knowledge was praiseworthy, not a few furnished solutions of special excellence. Both in the number of candidates who have succeeded and in the quality of their success pupils and teachers are to be congratulated.

ALGEBRA AND ARITHMETIC.

SENIOR GRADE.—BOYS AND GIRLS.

Report of FRANCIS A. TARLETON, LL.D., SC.D.

The answering in Algebra in the Senior Grade, compared with that in the Junior, shows in a striking manner the difficulty, peculiarly belonging to Mathematics, which meets the student in his progress

H

from elementary to more advanced knowledge. In the earlier stages of this progress the difficulty to a great extent results from the inability of many minds to understand the nature of the proof of a general theorem or to grasp the full import of algebraical processes. These retarding causes are fully exemplified in the answering in Algebra in the Senior Grade.

The number of girls presenting themselves for examination in this grade was too small for a fair comparison to be instituted between their answering and that of the boys, but I observed that the girls were more addicted to the pernicious habit of doing what they call "rough work," a practice which is exceedingly hostile to the attainment of high excellence.

In fact algebraical work if slovenly and imperfect is almost sure to give incorrect results, in which case it is worse than useless whilst, on the other hand, if it be sound and complete to copy it is needless waste of time and is liable to lead to error.

EUCLID.

SENIOR GRADE—BOYS.

Report of HENRY C. M'WEENEY, M.A.

The answering of the Senior Grade boys in Euclid was, on the whole, good. There were few failures and honour marks were obtained in a very large number of cases. The most prevalent error was the presenting of the demonstrations of certain Propositions in the Sixth Book, notably the Twenty-third, in a form altogether algebraical Euclid's reasoning being completely disregarded. Otherwise the candidates appear to have been well prepared, and they showed that they had had considerable practice in deductions.

SENIOR GRADE—GIRLS.

Report of ARTHUR A. RAMBAUT, M.A., SC.D.

The answering of the girls of the Senior Grade in Euclid was, on the whole, very good as is evidenced by the results viz., seventy-two per cent. passed and twenty-one per cent. with honours.

As a rule the questions from the book were done accurately and well but the fifth * and seventh questions appeared to give a great deal of trouble. In the seventh question especially, very few were able to give Euclid's definition of "Compound Ratio" correctly and many of those who did, by their proofs of Proposition VI., 23, in answer to the question, gave me the impression that they hardly grasped the meaning of the definition.

The deducibles were for the most part left severely alone.

* 5. Two triangles have an angle in each equal, and the sides about the equal angles reciprocally proportional. What can you infer about the triangles? Prove your statement.

MIDDLE GRADE.—BOYS.

Report of WM. F. TARTT, M.A.

On the whole, the answering on the Propositions was good and intelligent; I was specially pleased with the manner in which the boys seemed to have mastered the Sixth Book though many did not know how Euclid determines when four magnitudes are in proportion, and many were very confused over his method.

No. 4,[*] owing apparently to the manner of wording the question proved fatal to many. This points, no doubt, in some degree to learning by rote but still more, I think, to bad judgment: many simply quoted III., 36, as a reference, while, of course, the proof of this was required. Teachers, too, might do more in training their pupils to exercise judgment as to what reference and authorities they ought to quote when writing out the Propositions. Many boys wasted time in quoting Postulate or Axiom whenever they produced a line or advanced even the most elementary step in reasoning. Of course I do not wish to encourage incomplete answering but I think a Middle Grade boy ought to be able to recognise the main links in the chain of reasoning on which the Proposition depends and in giving the references for these I have no doubt he would satisfy any examiner.

Some teachers do not appear to be sufficiently careful in explaining the meaning of terms to their pupils. Many boys did not comprehend the meaning of the term "equimultiple," for example; and many said "take a *third* proportional" when they obviously meant "a mean proportional."

Several solved the deductions very well, and indeed elegantly; but very many did not attempt any of them.

The "Overage" boys were nearly all about the average: they knew the Propositions well, but they rarely attempted a deduction.

MIDDLE GRADE.—GIRLS.

Report of JOHN H. BERNARD, M.A., D.D.

I have to report that the answering in this subject was creditable and showed careful preparation. Only a small number of the candidates examined obtained honours; but, then, only a small number failed to obtain a pass. The papers were neatly worked, and the attempts to answer the problems were not unintelligent. The number of failures to answer correctly Euclid VI., i. was so large, that it would seem to indicate some defect in the teaching of Euclid's theory of proportion.

[*] A, P is a point within a circle of which O is the centre. Two straight lines AP'B, CPD, of which neither is perpendicular to PO, are drawn through P, meeting the circle in A, B, and C, D respectively. Prove that the rectangle contained by AP and PB is equal to the rectangle contained by CP and PD.

M 3

EUCLID.

JUNIOR GRADE.—BOYS OF THE PRESCRIBED AGE.

Report of RODERT W. GRIFFIN, M.A., LL.D., HENRY C. M'WEENEY, M.A., and STEPHEN B. KELLEHER, M.A.

The answering of the Junior Grade boys in Euclid was not satisfactory, over 40 per cent. failed, only about 15 per cent. obtained honour marks, and but 3 per cent. answered in a creditable manner. In very many instances there was a complete absence of method in writing out the demonstrations, and the examiners were greatly perplexed by the indiscriminate use of symbols and abbreviations, both those generally recognized and others, without any explanation of their meaning; it frequently happened that the same symbol was used in different senses, one in particular being made to do duty for 'square', 'parallelogram', and 'rectangle'. In many cases the figures were badly drawn, and the lettering on them could with difficulty be deciphered. There was very little judgment displayed in the quoting of authorities, unimportant ones being continually given and really essential ones omitted. It was a usual experience to be given the authority for joining two points, whereas in the 20th Proposition of the First Book the reference to the 12th Axiom was generally omitted.

JUNIOR GRADE.—BOYS—OVER-AGE.

Report of THOMAS W. INWOOD, B.A.

There was much uniformity in the standard reached by the over-age boys. Both very good papers and extremely bad ones were few in number. The standard reached, though not a high one, was decidedly creditable.

JUNIOR GRADE.—GIRLS.

Report of THOMAS W. INWOOD, B.A.

The answering of the girls in this grade cannot be considered quite satisfactory. A great many had evidently presented themselves for examination without anything like proper preparation. In some cases several pages were written for which not a single mark could be given. It would be well for students to realize that it is useless to try and get up a number of Propositions of Euclid without understanding the reasoning and method of the very early ones.

Most of those who knew their work wrote it out clearly and intelligently. There were, of course, cases of carelessness in lettering, of confusion in the use of the signs for "greater than" and "less than," and other similar errors. On the whole, however, this part of the work deserves commendation.

In proving I, 18, several of the students confined themselves to showing that the exterior angle is greater than one of the interior and opposite angles, though the word "each" was italicised in the question paper. A variation of the wording of a Proposition of the Second Book seems to have caused difficulty to many for the question was often neglected altogether and sometimes a Proposition was proved which had nothing to do with the question. In writing out II., 14, students constantly forgot to mention that the parallelogram first constructed should be right-angled. In connection with this it is important to point out that an examiner cannot accept for "rectangle" an abbreviation which is only recognised for "parallelogram." Students were asked in question 8 to construct on a given straight line a segment of a circle containing an angle equal to a given obtuse angle, but a very great many took no notice of the word "obtuse" or else in their figure drew an acute angle. In answering this question there was often a want of clearness as to which was the original given line and as to which was the required segment constructed.

Of the deductions given the first was proved correctly by a fair number, but the other three were very seldom attempted with any success. Comparatively few of the over age girls passed in this grade.

PREPARATORY GRADE.—BOYS.

Report of Rev. THOMAS R. POWER, ARTHUR A. RAMBAUT, M.A., SC.D., and WILLIAM E. THRIFT, M.A.

The result is in general satisfactory, and a high percentage of passes has been reached. Of those who failed, many appeared to have made no study or preparation and did not really attempt to answer any questions.

No doubt ridiculous blunders were plentiful, especially in defining a straight line, and the many absurd definitions put forward seem to indicate on the part of the teachers a disregard of the importance of impressing on the students a clear idea of the meaning of the terms they use.

In the sixth question very few were able to express intelligibly what they meant by the rectangle contained by two straight lines, and the indirect proof used in the second question (I., 14) was often imperfectly exhibited. Many candidates wasted a great deal of time in writing out the words of the questions. Many, too, seemed to think it necessary to place a different letter at each side of a line to represent a point upon it and in more than one case students have indicated a point where two lines meet by placing a separate letter in each of the four angles thus formed and have referred to the point by one or other of the four indifferently.

9. What is the nature of the figure formed by joining the middle points of the adjacent sides of any quadrilateral? Prove your statement. What would the figure so formed be called if the diagonals of the original quadrilateral were equal.

10. If the sum of the squares on the four sides of a quadrilateral is equal to the sum of the squares on the diagonals, prove that the quadrilateral is a parallelogram.

11. Construct a triangle being given the base, the sum of the sides, and the length of the perpendicular from one extremity of the base on the bisector of the external vertical angle.

12. One circle touches another internally. A chord of the outer circle touches the inner circle; prove that its segments subtend equal angles at the point of contact of the circles.

EUCLID.

Very few attempted the deductions* but those who did succeeded fairly and some few of them showed remarkable intelligence in their solutions, but only the very best were able to cope with the last question on the paper.

———

PREPARATORY GRADE—GIRLS.

Report of THOMAS W. INWOOD, B.A.

The work done by the girls in this grade was on the whole very satisfactory, for although many of those who failed had no knowledge whatsoever of the subject, yet on the other hand the number of really good papers was very considerable.

With regard to details, the definition of a straight line was seldom given correctly, but the propositions of the First Book were generally well known.

Students should notice carefully the order of Euclid's propositions in order to guard against a mistake which was often made, viz., that of taking the 19th proposition for granted when proving the 18th. Some candidates substituted the 29th for the 28th which was asked. It was not uncommon to find two angles spoken of as being two right angles when it ought to have been stated that they were equal to two right angles. Coming to the Second Book, very few explained clearly what is meant by "the rectangle contained by two straight lines." No doubt with some students this was due to inability to express themselves properly, but there were many cases of evident ignorance on the matter. It is obvious that absolute clearness on this point is necessary to a proper understanding of Book II. The propositions of this book were written out correctly by a large number of the candidates, but in constructions, when a straight line had to be drawn parallel to another, students did not always indicate through what point the former should be drawn.

A few successful attempts were made at the first three of the deductions*, but the last question seems to have presented almost insurmountable difficulty.

Time was often wasted in copying out the questions from the examination paper. It is quite sufficient to give the number of a question before answering it.

* 9. At any point X in the base BC of an isosceles triangle, ABC, a straight line is drawn perpendicular to the base meeting AB in E and AC produced in F, prove that the triangle AEF is isosceles.

10. If it is a parallelogram, ABCD, the side AB is bisected at E and the side DC at F, prove that the lines ED and FB are parallel to each other, and that they bisect the diagonal AC.

11. Prove that any two sides of a triangle are together greater than twice the straight line drawn from the middle point of the third side to the opposite vertex.

12. Being given two intersecting straight lines of indefinite length, find a point in one of them such that its distance from a fixed point in the same straight line shall be equal to its perpendicular distance from the other. How many such points can be found?

ALGEBRA.

MIDDLE GRADE.—BOYS.

Report of J. P. JOHNSTON, M.A.

The candidates in this Grade, were well acquainted with the particular principles and methods to be employed in the solution of nearly all the questions set, but were not familiar with the general methods of arrangement and the proper amount and kind of detail necessary to ensure accuracy. The number of instances in which questions were worked through by candidates who, in a certain sense, might be said to know how to do them, without the correct result being obtained, or only arrived at after repeated attempts, was very large. In the question on division, in which some multiplication was necessary unless it was done by finding the factors of the dividend, a method rarely employed, it was quite common to find after the multiplication had been performed, very often not correctly, that the candidate proceeded to divide without re-arranging the terms in a definite order or even collecting together terms only differing by a numerical factor. Many other instances of a want of knowledge of the proper methods of working might be given.

The problems were answered correctly by a large number of students and they displayed considerable facility in finding the equations upon which the solution depended. Sufficient explanation was not always given of the way in which the equations were arrived at.

The work of the over-age candidates was very bad.

MIDDLE GRADE.—GIRLS.

Report of P. A. E. DOWLING, B.A.

The answering of the girls on this paper was, everything considered, fair and the results would have been much higher, in the vast majority of cases, were it not that many marks were lost owing to considerable inaccuracy, partly the result of the very long methods employed and the general absence of any attempt at concise manipulation.

In many cases the answering of some of the questions would indicate that, though the students could solve questions in Algebra, they knew very little of the principles of Algebra involved in the solutions.

JUNIOR GRADE.— BOYS OF THE PRESCRIBED AGE.

Report of GEORGE J. ALLMAN, D.SC., PATRICK KELLY, and FRANCIS A. TARLETON, LL.D., &C.D.

A large proportion of the candidates failed to obtain pass marks, and in this respect the answering was not satisfactory. The answering of those who passed was on the whole very good, several candidates having obtained full marks and a large number 75 per cent. or upwards.

We noticed that in the division of one polynomial by another many boys did not arrange the expressions according to powers of the same letter and failed in consequence to obtain a correct result.

We also observed that in attempting to solve an equation some boys obtained an expression for the unknown quantity involving itself and seemed to think that they had effected a solution.

JUNIOR GRADE.—BOYS.—OVER-AGE.

Report of JOHN H. BERNARD, M.A., D.D.

The answering in this subject of the over-age boys who presented themselves was decidedly bad. The paper was not too hard, as the answering of the girls proves; and the large number of failures can only be set down to the fault of the candidates. It must, at the same time, be borne in mind that the answering of over-age candidates is generally below the average.

JUNIOR GRADE.—GIRLS.

Report of JOHN H. BERNARD, M.A., D.D.

The answering was tolerably good in this department. Two candidates obtained full marks, which is a satisfactory indication that the paper was not of excessive difficulty. The failures were most conspicuous in Questions 3, 4, and 5; and suggest that great care and patience on the part of teachers are necessary if the theory of algebraic fractions is to be understood by the pupils.

PREPARATORY GRADE.—BOYS.

Report of WILLIAM BROOK, M.A., P. A. E. DOWLING, B.A., and J. P. JOHNSTON, M.A.

The answering in this Grade was very good; the work, in general, being both accurate and neat. The high answering is due in a great measure to this for the harder questions at the end of the paper were, in most cases, done by ordinary multiplication and division which entailed a considerable amount of long work, the shorter and more usual methods being seldom adopted, which is perhaps not to be wondered at when the age of the candidates is considered.

It would be well if students' attention were directed to the advisability, in questions like number 5, of obtaining the quotient according to powers of one of the terms. Very often in this question no order was observed.

Though the work as a whole was very satisfactory, in some instances the right answer was obtained though the work was wrong. In division questions it was common to find when a mistake had been made in the beginning of the work, in order that no remainder should be left, wrong signs or terms removed at the very end.

PREPARATORY GRADE.—GIRLS.

Report of WILLIAM BROOK, M.A.

The answering was very creditable, the work neat and accurate. Exception must, however, be taken to the attempts made to solve Question 3. The result arrived at was, in a great many instances, very absurd. The correct answer to Question 5 was obtained by a large number of candidates, but the method employed was generally too long.

ARITHMETIC.

MIDDLE GRADE.—BOYS AND GIRLS.

Report of J. J. BROWNE.

The work of the boys in this grade was satisfactory on the whole, that of the girls weak, and of the average candidate, boys and girls, weaker still.

The most general defect in the work was a want of neatness and clearness. Neatness and order undoubtedly have a considerable value in marks, although indirectly. A student who takes the trouble to set down his work in an orderly manner is generally accurate and ensures a correct result without losing time by working his questions in the rough; he can very easily revise his questions; and last though not least the examiner is able to follow his work, and allow him credit for anything of value he has done, even though he has made mistakes, or left the question unfinished. It should also be remembered that even when the result is correct the work must be such as the examiner can follow; and if the work of a question (even where only a single answer is required) naturally divides itself into steps, the result of each step should be clearly set forth in its place in the work. Far too much time was given to working in the rough and none, or nearly none, to verification.

With regard to defects of knowledge they were exhibited principally on fundamental points in the Middle Grade course proper. The difference between commercial and theoretical discount was much misunderstood. In Question 11 a gain of 10 per cent on the sale of 100 apples was very frequently set down as a gain of 10 per cent. The majority of candidates were ignorant of how a stockbroker's charge is calculated, even for Government stock. Some calculated it on the purchase money, others allowed the broker only one half-crown for the purchase of £4,760 stock, while many thought that the ½ per cent. brokerage converted the 2½ per cent. into 2¾ or 2¼ per cent. In fact mistakes were made on this point in greater variety than one would have thought possible. A mistake that was also of frequent occurrence was to confound income from an investment in stock, with the proceeds of the sale of the stock. In this matter of stocks and indeed in many other parts of the paper, a little common sense of the plainest kind would have been of great use to many candidates.

Many candidates solved questions by Algebraic methods, and for these they got little or no credit.

JUNIOR GRADE.—BOYS OF THE PRESCRIBED AGE.

Report of DANIEL FARRELLY and Rev. JOHN MAGWYN, LL.D.

In reading in our Report on the answering in Arithmetic of the Junior Grade boys of the prescribed age, we desire to say that, on the whole, the answering was fairly satisfactory. As was to be expected, the answering was much weaker in the questions that required to be carefully weighed and turned over in the mind than in those in which the application of mere practical rules sufficed, for the most part, to bring about the solution.

ARITHMETIC.

The papers, in general, were fairly written. Some faults, of course, occasionally cropped up. A few boys, when they came to the foot of the page on which they had commenced an exercise, turned back and filled up every blank spot, on the same page, with figures and lines, the figures growing smaller as the spaces, or spaces, were growing fewer, so that, by this means, the first part of the solution became almost last in position, on the paper; and the answer, or last part, first; or, what was still worse, it might be found sometimes half-buried in well nigh invisible symbols in the very heart of the black and unsightly entanglement that had thus been produced. We need hardly say that we think this practice deserves reproof.

Moreover, very clumsy and roundabout processes were now and then employed, with injurious results, in questions in fractions and proportion, and even in practice and interest. But, notwithstanding the drawbacks we have indicated, it is our firm conviction that the knowledge of arithmetic displayed by the present candidates generally, is very far in advance of what was exhibited by those who were examined by the Intermediate Education Board in the earlier years of its existence; and there was ample evidence to hand that many of the schools of the country are doing high-class work in this most important and serviceable branch of education.

JUNIOR GRADE.—BOYS.—OVER-AGE.

Report of Rev. THOMAS SUTCLIFFE, M.A.

Of the over-age boys examined in this grade about 77 per cent. passed; 36 per cent. obtained honour marks. Questions which could be solved mechanically were very generally done, but those requiring thought were, in too many cases, left unattempted or hopelessly bungled. The answering on the whole was very fair.

JUNIOR GRADE.—GIRLS.

Report of DANIEL FARRELLY.

Of the 1,010 girls whose work I have examined, 932 were within the prescribed age. Many of these obtained honours, 3 answered all the questions, 49 others scored between 400 and 600 marks, and very nearly 30 per cent. were rejected.

As to the 87 over-age students, only 17 or 19·6 per cent. were failures. To my mind it is far from unsatisfactory that girls are able to secure, in the subject of arithmetic, such results as these. Their attainments in this branch, so far as this grade is concerned, are evidently not very much inferior to those of the boys who belong to the same standard. In the joint report of Dr. Macbeth and myself upon the boys we examined, the quarter in which their answering, as a rule, was most robust is pointed out. What was said there in connexion with this feature may, with equal appropriateness, be said here of the girls.

A good many of the candidates attempted to simplify fractional quantities by clumsy and unmethodical operations. They spent themselves fruitlessly in the effort to unravel, more or less, at each step, all the parts of the question together, instead of operating upon it piecemeal and reducing its links, one by one, to a few simple factors for the close.

ARITHMETIC.

I am not one to pass a sweeping condemnation on clumsy methods generally, for they are often due to the excitement of an examination and to the brief time that can be spared for reflection, and they sometimes indicate in the candidate much depth and power. But there are places where such methods point to inferior teaching and call for censure. Again, in proportional arithmetic, including interest, some attempts, necessarily burdensome, were made, but, in almost every instance in vain, to effect solutions by means of what is called the "Unit Method." It seems to me that it would be very much better for candidates to master the principles of proportion and leave this method of "Reduction to the Unit" to its own proper domain to do service there.

A pretty large number were unable to express, as a decimal or simple number, the decimal fraction $\frac{147}{1000}$ which came up in the solution of one of the exercises, by the simple and usual process of writing only the numerator and indicating, by the proper position of the decimal point left of it, the value of the denominator. Being evidently not grounded in the notation of decimals, they unnecessarily entangled themselves in tedious, and, to many of them, as their work proved, difficult and hurtful courses. They reduced the decimal fraction to the equivalent vulgar one $\frac{1}{125}$, and eventually did not succeed in converting this vulgar fraction to the decimal required. There were also those who seemed to have had no training whatever in "Short Division" or in the use of factors, even where their help, as in the multiplication of large compound numbers, could not well be done without. The arithmetical efforts of such students are usually erroneous, always painfully roundabout, and, owing probably to careless teaching, characterised, more or less, by mental feebleness. The answering was not as general as one might reasonably expect in the questions that were set in practice and in interest.

The defects above enumerated were the principal ones that came under my notice. But it must now be said that, to a fair extent, the girls' papers were turned out most creditably—solutions neat, concise, and clever, showing, beyond question, that the candidates were taught with great care and ability, and that the schools from which they came are doing excellent work for their pupils in this part of their studies.

PREPARATORY GRADE.—BOYS.

Report of J. J. BROWNE, Rev. THOMAS SUTCLIFFE, B.A., and FREDERICK A. WHITTON.

With the exception of a small proportion of obviously unprepared candidates, we found the answering in general very satisfactory, and it displayed considerable intelligence.

The failures were, as usual, principally in the cases requiring exercise of the reasoning faculties, and in some instances roundabout methods were adopted, where shorter and more direct means were available; for instance, in division of decimals the very clumsy plan of arranging for the points by adding ciphers to the divisor was very common. In simplification of vulgar fractions few candidates showed a correct knowledge of combining or grouping the parts together, and in the important matter of notation, both of integers and decimals, a remarkable amount of ignorance was exhibited. Also, when using the sign of subtraction to indicate the difference between two quantities the wrong quantity was constantly put first. In long, and even in short, division a cipher occurring in the quotient was frequently left out.

Although it was quite common to find the questions worked out twice (first in the rough), it is somewhat remarkable that very few attempts were made to verify the result by a converse process.

Neatness and order were frequently exhibited, especially by those obtaining the highest marks, but many candidates lost considerably by the want of them.

Marks are given for any valuable work that the Examiner can follow, even though the question is left unfinished or an incorrect result arrived at, but where the work is a mere jumble of figures marks are inevitably lost. Marks to a considerable extent were lost through mistakes in copying from the printed paper and from the candidate's own work. Students should remember that all necessary work should appear on the ruled side of the paper though the question may have been done in the rough on the unruled side.

In some instances students either failed to number their answers or placed wrong numbers opposite them.

——

PREPARATORY GRADE.—GIRLS.

Report of Rev. THOMAS SUTCLIFFE, B.A.

The answering in this grade was unsatisfactory. Only 21 per cent. obtained honour marks, and 43 per cent. failed altogether. This result is largely owing to inaccuracy in the students' work. In this particular the girls were far worse than the boys. The great majority of the girls failed to obtain credit for the question in simple notation, and very few, not 10 per cent., made an intelligent attempt to work the two questions which required some thought. There were, of course, some very good papers, one girl using fractions in a way which showed great promise. But, on the whole, the answering was not good and the great blot was inaccuracy.

——

BOOK-KEEPING.

MIDDLE GRADE.—BOYS AND GIRLS.

Report of FREDERICK A. WHITTON.

The answering of both boys and girls in this Grade has improved in my opinion, and the candidates are apparently better prepared. The proportion of boys obtaining honour marks has increased and there has also been an improvement in this respect in the case of the girls, though not to the same extent.

The execution of the work was in most cases highly creditable, that of the boys generally being rather better than the girls.

Junior Grade.—Boys and Girls.

Report of Frederick A. Whitton.

The answering in this Grade was fairly good, the proportion of failures being about 25 per cent. of the boys, and 16 per cent. of the girls. Of those who passed a larger number should, I think, have obtained honour marks.

In the Journal portion of the paper, the ordinary simple transactions were almost invariably correctly recorded, but the entries requiring some exercise of thought were seldom all properly made. In some cases students omitted these entries altogether.

A bad form of journalising was noticeable in several instances, such as placing the debit and credit upon the line, leaving no line between each entry, etc.

Some students also left themselves without sufficient time to complete the paper by copying out Question 3, involving some twenty lines of wholly unnecessary manuscript, instead of proceeding at once to journalise the transactions.

A few others disregarded the plain instructions, printed on the covers of their Answer-Books, to be careful to use the pages suited to the work set them.

I am glad to be able to report that neatness and care, so essential in Book-keeping, generally characterised the execution of the work of both boys and girls.

NATURAL PHILOSOPHY.

Senior Grade.—Boys and Girls.

Report of A. W. Scott, M.A.

I have examined the Answer-Books in Natural Philosophy of 65 Senior Grade boys. Although the percentage of failures is less, they have not done so well as those in the Middle Grade. Many of the candidates appeared to have got up portions here and there, which they expected to be set, without studying the subject thoroughly. Thus, some evidently expected that "Faraday's Ice-Pail" would be asked and immediately produced it when a question appeared in order to ascertain if they knew Faraday's experimental proof that electricity resides on the outer surface of a conductor, forgetting that their answer in the form in which they presented it showed that, under certain circumstances, electricity can reside on the inside of a hollow conductor. Many common pieces of apparatus were not known at all; but few described the Thermopile correctly, although many attempted it, and no one knew why a Galvanometer of low resistance must be used with this instrument. The general impression I formed was that most of the candidates had got up their work only from books, that it was imperfectly prepared, and that they wrote the least amount which they thought would satisfy the Examiner. A few of the best boys wrote good papers and in some cases illustrated the subject with neat diagrams. The papers of six girls in this grade (who all passed) call for no special comment.

NATURAL PHILOSOPHY.

MIDDLE GRADE.—BOYS AND GIRLS.

Report of A. W. SCOTT, M.A.

I have examined the answer books in Natural Philosophy of 132 Middle Grade boys, and I am satisfied with the result. The opinion I have formed is that on the whole they have reached a fair average and that many have acquired a useful knowledge of the subject. Good descriptions of the gas-engine and neat drawings of the cylinder of a steam-engine, showing the action of the slide-valves, were given by some of the candidates. I was surprised to find how very few of those who correctly described the construction of a thermometer, were aware that the boiling point of the steam from boiling water varies with the height of the barometer, and that the determination of the upper of the standard points as they described it could only give a correct result by accident. I was pleased to find that question 9, the hardest on the paper, was done correctly by several, while the answers of some more only required to be multiplied by 2, Joule's equivalent having been given for Fahrenheit degrees, while 80, the number assumed for the latent heat of fusion, was for 1 degree centigrade. Many do not appear to read the questions carefully. In question 3 (b) the word "slightly" ought to have suggested that the phenomena of "heats" would occur, yet very few answered it correctly. Full marks were obtained for each question by some one or other of the candidates, from which I infer that the standard was not too high. Four girls, who all passed, sent in papers in this grade, three did creditably.

JUNIOR GRADE.—BOYS AND GIRLS.

Report of JOHN BURKE, M.A.

The average answering was, on the whole, an improvement upon that of last year, but that of the best candidates was of an inferior type.

The ordinary stock questions which required nothing but memory to answer were replied to often in most lucid terms but in a number of cases, which were no doubt exceptions, were such as to suggest that they were not the candidate's own version but merely a recitation of something previously committed to memory. On the other hand, those questions which were perhaps at first sight not quite so familiar, but which nevertheless were probably simpler, requiring merely a knowledge of fundamental principles and only a little thought, were seldom correctly answered. For instance, whilst the question relating to stable, unstable, and neutral equilibrium was answered rightly by a very large number indeed the answer to the one on the Magdeburg hemispheres was given correctly only by a few, a favourite notion being that the two equal and opposite forces of 180 lbs. each should be added in submitting the answer. Again amongst the answers to the question about a man walking on a level road the idea seemed prevalent that no work would be done by him, unless he were to lift his centre of gravity.

It was of course assumed in the question that the work which would be done in going up a slight incline of 1 in 20, supposing gravity did not act, would be the same as that of walking on a level ground ; so that

If double the work be done in walking up an incline of 1 in 20, against gravity, as in walking the same distance along a level road, the work done in the latter case would be equal to lifting the man's weight through a height of $\frac{1}{20}$th of the distance.

A very common error also was to suppose that if the force of gravity were doubled the number of vibrations of a simple pendulum would also be doubled.

In the cricket ball question the first part was usually answered correctly, but in the determination of the distance horizontally to which the ball would have travelled before striking the ground, hopeless confusion almost invariably arose by the introduction of every imaginable formula, where all that was required to be known was that the horizontal component of the velocity of the ball remained constant, and that the time of flight was two seconds, which followed immediately from the first part. The correct answer, 30 feet, was given by not more than half-a-dozen candidates.

It may once more be pointed out, how very inadvisable it is to make, especially very young students, attempt to acquire a knowledge of physics by merely committing a host of facts, formulæ and definitions to memory; surely, if something is required for them to exercise their memory with, wholesome food may be found in the study of Greek verbs or the like. But in the study of nature it is not at all desirable to tax the memory thus, because here it can only be done at the expense of crushing the powers of observation and the inventive faculty, which, though undoubtedly are possessed in different degrees by different students, are nevertheless given in some extent at least, to all, and it is their faculties in particular that the teacher of science should be ever mindful to unfold. If people persist in teaching science, as though it were a mere compendium of facts, &c., its value as a branch of education could not but be ultimately ignored.

There is no time of life where those qualities which are so essential to a scientific mind can be so easily drawn out as in early youth, when that boyish enthusiasm, that childish spirit of inquiry that demands the why and the wherefore for everything, can be so fruitfully watched over and encouraged. To excite curiosity in the phenomena around us ought to be the guiding principle in the teaching of science; and in proportion as a person creates a real interest in everything that comes before the mind of his pupil, is he as a teacher of science a success or a failure.

I would venture to suggest that as religious communities with good sense are ever mindful to guard over the religious and moral instincts of children, so also ought those who have the progress of science at heart to insist upon the proper development of that attitude of mind which conduces to scientific habits of thought and to secure that the scientific instincts will not be rooted out of the mind of our youth when they are just beginning to bud. When these instincts have been extinguished by a deliberate effort not to think, all we may hope to obtain are living phonographs, measuring rods, and calculating machines, but not scientific men.

It ought therefore to be sufficient to appeal to the moral sense of the teacher to secure that those qualities of youth upon which the scientific worth and work of the future will so much depend—without which the study of science becomes a farce equivalent to its real neglect—will not ultimately be effaced by error.

CHEMISTRY.

JUNIOR, MIDDLE, AND SENIOR GRADES.—BOYS AND GIRLS.

Report of WALTER E. ADENEY, A.B.C.SC.I., F.I.C.

Those parts of the papers of questions which required simple book knowledge, including arithmetical exercises, to answer, were, on the whole, well done. There was, however, very little indication that the candidates had received any systematic instruction in Experimental and Practical Chemistry. It was not surprising, therefore, to find that the answers to questions requiring intelligent thought were generally extremely weak. The majority of the candidates possessed no intelligent conceptions of the fundamental principles covered by the terms— "atomic weight," "equivalent," and "atomicity."

No candidate gave an explanation of the "relation of the density of a gas to its molecular weight" (Junior Grade, No. 4).

The candidates also appeared ignorant of the volume and weight relationships indicated by the molecular formulæ of gaseous substances.

The questions in Practical Chemistry, set for the Middle and Senior Grades, brought out the fact that the candidates, with a few, it is pleasant to be able to report, marked exceptions, had no real knowledge of that most important branch of the subject.

I do not remember a single candidate having fully answered the question—" Explain how the formula CO for carbon dioxide has been adduced " (Senior Grade, No. 1), although the question ought to have proved very simple to a senior pupil.

It is much to be regretted, I consider, that the attention of the pupils in the Intermediate schools of the country appears to be so little directed to the experimental and practical study of Chemistry.

The worked papers this year afford ample evidence of earnest effort, both on the part of teacher and pupil, to make up the book work; but such efforts can scarcely be regarded as of much educational value. Were they supplemented, however, by an adequate study of Experimental and Practical Chemistry, the educational value which would follow them would be of very great value; and, in addition, such courses of practical study would afford an invaluable training to those pupils, who afterwards enter the medical or other scientific professions, or follow agriculture or other technical industrial pursuits.

DRAWING.

OBJECT DRAWING.

SENIOR GRADE.—BOYS AND GIRLS.

Report of GEORGE M. ATKINSON.

Many of the exercises show a want of preliminary study in model drawing. In several cases there is evidence of ignorance of the principles of perspective, and sufficient attention is not given to the details of the objects, and to the correct rendering of the forms of the shadows. The group was set to test the candidates' powers of observation as well as their executive skill. Some only drew the outline of the objects, these were so far satisfactory, and by application they may on another occasion obtain better results.

PERSPECTIVE AND PROJECTION OF SHADOWS, ETC.

SENIOR GRADE.—BOYS AND GIRLS.

Report of THOMAS SCULLY, R.H.

In this grade the performance of both boys and girls was shamefully bad, as would usually seem to be the case. This state of things, I think, can only be explained by the theory that the students have reached an age when they begin to question the ultimate utility of these subjects, with results fatal to progress, naturally, therefore the number of students taking up these subjects is always small. The questions set were exceedingly simple, yet their treatment was miserable.

In perspective, questions 1 and 2, here quoted :—

"PERSPECTIVE.

[The height of the eye is 5 feet above ground plane, the distance of the spectator from the picture plane is 12 feet and the scale is ½ inch to 1 foot.]

1. A line cuts the picture plane 3 feet to the left, and 5 feet above the ground line, and the ground plane 3 feet to the right and 10 feet behind the picture plane. Place in perspective, and show a construction to determine the middle point of the portion of this line intercepted between the picture plane and the ground plane.

2. A line cuts the picture plane 2 feet to the right and 5 feet above the ground line, and the ground plane 4 feet to the left and 8 feet behind the picture plane. Place in perspective, and show a construction to get the perspective representation of the line bisecting the angle between the given line and the ground plane."

are of an elementary nature and admit of an immediate and simple solution, their peculiarity being that the students could not solve them unless they really understood the principle of perspective, yet the result was that scarcely a single satisfactory answer was given to these questions.

All the remaining questions were commonplace and simple, yet their treatment was contemptible.

———

FREEHAND.

MIDDLE GRADE.—BOYS.

Report of A. W. FENTON LANGMAN.

The drawings, as a whole, were fairly satisfactory, nearly 20 per cent. obtaining very high marks.

The following points should, however, be noted and avoided in the future, viz. :—Hurried lining-in which neutralize much of the good work in the preliminary sketch, and drawing leaves by their edges first instead of carefully interpreting the forms of the leading ribs.

MIDDLE GRADE.—GIRLS.

Report of A. W. FENTON LANGMAN.

A good average is shown by the papers examined.

In many cases there is a marked tendency to draw the copy in piece, instead of setting out the main lines, on both sides, with their proper proportions between the given limits, and then clothing these with the minor forms.

The principle of working one-half of the copy is a bad one, as it leads to an incorrect analysis of the example given.

It is very satisfactory to find there are very few really bad papers.

PRACTICAL GEOMETRY.

MIDDLE GRADE.—BOYS.

Report of P. J. PRENDERGAST, A.M.I.C.E.

Some very good exercises were submitted, but the average result of the work done cannot be considered satisfactory, while that of the "over-age" candidates was very poor.

MIDDLE GRADE.—GIRLS.

Report of P. J. PRENDERGAST, A.M.I.C.E.

The general answering of the girls in this grade is more satisfactory than that of the boys. The exercises, on the whole, showed a fair knowledge of the subject, but the answering of the "over-age" candidates was most disappointing.

FREEHAND.

JUNIOR GRADE.—BOYS.

Report of A. W. FENTON LANGMAN.

This set of works is exceedingly creditable, and there is a very large number of first-class drawings. The results show excellent teaching.

In some cases there is great constructive weakness, and the spacing is poor.

In many drawings a proper estimate of a good line is maintained, but not at the expense of good form. This is as it should be and is worthy of commendation.

JUNIOR GRADE.—GIRLS.

Report of THOMAS SCULLY, B.E.

The work done in this grade is, generally speaking, featureless and the standard of proficiency is much below that of the Preparatory Grade in the same subject. The study was easy, yet there was not a single example of really good work.

PRACTICAL GEOMETRY.

JUNIOR GRADE.—BOYS.

Report of P. J. PRENDERGAST, A.M.I.C.E.

The answering in Practical Geometry by the Junior Grade boys was very satisfactory. Many of the exercises were of a very high standard and displayed careful preparation as well as sound teaching.

Some of the candidates failed to obtain full credit for solutions in which the constructions lines were not shown, although expressly warned to that effect by a note on the Examination Paper.

JUNIOR GRADE.—GIRLS.

Report of THOMAS SCULLY, B.E.

The majority of students in this grade showed a fair knowledge of the subject as far as the portion dealing with Plane Geometry is concerned but the treatment of the Solid Geometry was decidedly weak. There were, however, some very good papers and no more bad ones than might be expected amongst such a large number of young students.

FREEHAND.

PREPARATORY GRADE.—BOYS.

Report of GEORGE M. ATKINSON.

I have pleasure in reporting that I find the exercises on the whole quite equal to last year's work ; the greater portion showed evidence of fair teaching, the constructing lines were fairly shown, and a large number received high marks and were well able to execute the example set.

There are not many failures, and most of these are due to negligence and simple carelessness on the part of the candidates, not want of ability, for one finds one part of the example well done and other portions neglected, of course these candidates suffered in consequence.

I 2

PREPARATORY GRADE.—GIRLS.

Report of THOMAS SCULLY, B.E.

The study for this grade was by no means easy, but on the whole the students treated the subject well. The examples of very inferior work were not many, and the best paper, to which I have given full marks, is a really creditable piece of work for so young a student. On the whole, I think this grade has treated the subject with advantage.

MUSIC.

JUNIOR, MIDDLE, AND SENIOR GRADES.—GIRLS ONLY.

Report of J. CHRISTOPHER MARKS, MUS. D.

In the Junior Grade the answering all round was fair and, in some cases, excellent, more attention was paid to inserting the key signatures and accidentals than formerly, but still a large number neglected to attend to this very simple and important matter.

In the Middle Grade, the papers on the whole were excellent.

In the Senior Grade, with the exception of the History section, the answering was disappointing, the counterpoint was weak, and the answers to the Harmony questions, with a few exceptions, were not creditable.

SHORTHAND.

JUNIOR, MIDDLE, AND SENIOR GRADES—BOYS AND GIRLS.

Report of HENRY HOLT and CHARLES RYAN.

The Junior Boys' answering in A paper was, in some cases, very good, the shorthand very neatly and accurately written, evidencing careful teaching and study of the system. To this general statement, however, there are many exceptions, some candidates, even including some who wrote the entire, or nearly the entire, of the paper, having consulted gross inaccuracies, as well as manifesting a general carelessness and slovenliness in writing, and we had in consequence to make serious deductions from the number of marks to which they would otherwise have been entitled. There is no doubt this was due to insufficient preparation, and several boys stated at the end of their papers, as a reason for special consideration, that they had been only learning shorthand for three or four weeks. The leading error seemed to be the misplacement of the hooks. In the B paper the answering of the candidates was for the most part excellent, many of them scoring over 100 marks, out of a possible 150, on this paper alone. Some would have obtained the full number of marks, were it not for defects in spelling, punctuation and neatness of hand-writing. These are matters to which more attention on the part of candidates is desirable. Speed in the writing of shorthand is of course very important, but no amount of mere speed can compensate for lack of neatness in transcribing notes into longhand or for faulty spelling and punctuation which are essential in order to entitle a candidate to full marks. On the whole, the Junior candidates acquitted themselves creditably. There were 641 Junior boys examined, of those 326 passed, and 216 failed. Among the girls 26 passed and 18 failed. In the Middle Grade it was quite clear that the candidates were, with one or two exceptions, students who had passed in the Junior Grade in the previous year and had improved in the meantime, for they were all either very good or, as indicative of a first attempt, very bad. Both A and B papers were done in full by several students. In the Middle Grade there was a noticeable inability on the part of the candidates to accommodate themselves to some very ordinary contractions. Of eighty-six boys in this grade, sixty-one passed and twenty-five failed. Of the girls four passed and two failed.

In the Senior Grade, in the case of those who failed, there was evidenced a very serious want of preparation, and in some instances the work done was such as would not have entitled the candidates to pass even in the Junior or Middle Grades. Some of them had apparently devoted only a few weeks to the study of the system. Fifteen boys presented themselves for examination; of these twelve passed (three with honours) and three failed. There were only two girls to be examined, one passed and one failed.

BOTANY.

JUNIOR, MIDDLE, AND SENIOR GRADES.—GIRLS ONLY.

Report of ALEXANDER BLAYNEY, M.A., M.B.

As this is the first time I have had the examination in Botany entrusted to me, I am unable to say how the answering compares with that of former years. However, judging from the report on last year's examination, I should say that the preparation for this subject still continues to be deficient mainly on one most important point —*practical* instruction. It consists merely of a close study of the recommended text-book in Botany while no trouble has been taken to acquire a knowledge of the appearance of even the commonest flowers belonging to the prescribed orders. I was particularly struck with this when reading many papers in which excellent answers were given to the questions on the meaning of botanical terms or on the general structure of plants, but most disappointing and meagre were the descriptions of flowers in nearly all cases. The almost invariable rule was when the description of a particular flower was required to find one given which might apply to any flower in the whole natural order of which it was only one member, while the peculiarities of the individual flower were scarcely in a single instance correctly answered. This method of study is particularly to be regretted in the case of Botany. There is no other subject in the Intermediate course which affords such excellent opportunity for developing the power of accurate observation, but as at present taught it serves only to put a further strain on the, in many cases, already overburthened memory.

Speaking of individual grades, the proportions of passes formed an ascending series from Junior to Senior, and while the general level of the answering was higher in the Senior than in the Middle, and in the Middle than in the Junior, in the latter there were a few papers which reached a much higher standard than was attained in either of the remaining grades. On the whole there was evidence of much attentive study and considerable intelligence.

BOYS.

List of Schools to the Managers of which Sunday Fees were Paid in 18.., and Amount of each Fee—continued

GIRLS.

Parish	Town	Name of School									
		Brought forward									

List of Returns to the Managers of each Sunday School Fair ... Paid in 187 ... and Amount of each Recommended

TABLE

Parish	Name	School Attend.	Total number in attendance	Total amount raised	Total Amount Recommended

List of Schools to the Managers of which Results Fees were Paid in 1871, and Amounts of each Fee—continued

OTHER.

County	Town	Name of School									

CORK.

CONTINUED.

APPENDIX V.

Localities in which Examinations were held.

BOYS.

Localities	No. of Centres	Localities	No. of Centres
Abbeyleix,	1	Kilrush,	1
Armagh,	2	Kingstown,	2
Athenry,	1	Letterkenny,	1
Athlone,	1	Limerick,	6
Athy,	1	Lisburn,	1
Ballaghaderreen,	1	Lismore,	1
Ballinrobe,	1	Listowel,	1
Ballymena,	2	Londonderry,	3
Ballymoney,	1	Longford,	1
Bangor,	1	Lurgan,	1
Belfast,	18	Mallow,	1
Blackrock,	6	Midleton,	2
Bruff,	1	Mitchelstown,	1
Caherciveen,	1	Monaghan,	2
Callan,	1	Mount Bellew,	1
Carlow,	2	Mountrath,	1
Carrick-on-Suir,	1	Mullingar,	2
Cashel,	6	Multyfarnham,	1
Castlebar,	2	Naas,	1
Cavan,	1	Navan,	1
Charleville,	1	Nenagh,	1
Clongowes Wood College,	3	Newbridge,	1
Clonmel,	2	New Ross,	1
Clontarf,	1	Newry,	3
Clones,	1	Omagh,	1
Coleraine,	1	Parsonstown,	1
Cookstown,	1	Portarlington,	1
Cork,	18	Queenstown,	1
Dingle,	1	Raphoe,	1
Drogheda,	2	Rathmines,	1
Dublin,	40	Roscommon,	1
Dundalk,	3	Rosscarbery,	1
		Skibbereen,	1
Dungannon,	2	Sligo,	3
Dungarvan,	1	Strabane,	1
Ennis,	2	Tarbert,	1
Enniscorthy,	1	Thurles,	1
Enniskillen,	2	Tipperary,	1
Ennistymon,	1	Tralee,	2
Fermoy,	3	Tramore,	1
Galway,	2	Tuam,	2
Holywood (Down),	1	Waterford,	5
Kells,	1	Westport,	1
Kilkenny,	3	Wexford,	3
Killarney,	1	Youghal,	1
		Total,	192

Localities in which Examinations were held—*continued.*
GIRLS.

Localities	No. of Centres	Localities	No. of Centres
Armagh,	1	Killarney,	1
Athy,	1	Letterkenny,	1
Balbriggan,	1	Limerick,	2
Ballymena,	1	Lisburn,	1
Ballymoney,	1	Londonderry,	3
Ballyshannon,	1	Longford,	1
Belfast,	10	Monaghan,	1
Blackrock,	1	Mountmellick,	1
Bray,	1	Mullingar,	1
Carrickfergus,	1	Navan,	1
Chapelizod,	1	New Ross,	1
Cork,	5	Newry,	1
Dalkey,	1	Omagh,	1
Dublin,	13	Portadown,	1
Dungannon,	1	Rathfarnham,	1
Enniscorthy,	1	Sligo,	2
Galway,	1	Thurles,	1
Gorey,	1	Tralee,	1
Holywood (Down),	1	Waterford,	2
Kilkenny,	1	Wexford,	1
		Total,	71

APPENDIX VI.

THE BURKE MEMORIAL PRIZES.

A sum of money, subscribed in memory of the late THOMAS HENRY BURKE, Esq., Under Secretary to the Lord Lieutenant, was transferred by the Burke Memorial Committee, on 18th March, 1884, to the Intermediate Education Board for Ireland, who undertook to administer the Fund in accordance with the following Rules—(the sum funded is £1,922 16s. 11d. Consols):—

I. The annual income from the fund shall be applied in paying three Prizes, one of £16, one of £10, and a second of £10 ; any surplus or deficiency to be apportioned in the same ratio. If, in the opinion of the Commissioners, sufficient merit be not shown by the Candidates competing to justify the award of any or either of the Prizes, the amount of such Prize may be, at the discretion of the Board, withheld and added to the principal.

II. No student shall be qualified to receive these Prizes except the children of persons who are, or have been, in receipt of salary or pension in Ireland, paid out of money derived from Parliamentary Grants, Rates or Taxes, other than members of the Naval or Military Services, not being also in Civil employment.

III. The Prizes shall be awarded as follows :—that of £16 to the Boy whom, at the annual Examination in the Junior Grade among Male Candidates qualified in the manner expressed in the next preceding Rule, the Board shall adjudge to rank highest in answering ; One Prize of £10 to the Boy whom in the same Grade at such Examination the Board shall adjudge to rank second among such persons in answering ; and the other of £10 to the Girl whom, at such Examination in the same Grade, among Female Candidates qualified in the manner aforesaid, the Board shall adjudge to rank highest in answering.

IV. The decision of the Board shall be final and decisive in determining whether the Candidates fulfil the conditions of the third Rule.

V. The Board may deduct all expenses connected with the trust from the yearly income.

No. 1521.

DUBLIN CASTLE,

11th March, 1898.

GENTLEMEN,

I have to acknowledge the receipt of your letter of the 9th instant, forwarding, for submission to His Excellency the Lord Lieutenant, the Report of the Intermediate Education Board for Ireland for the year 1897.

I am,

Gentlemen,

Your obedient Servant,

(Signed),   D. HARREL.

The Assistant Commissioners of
    Intermediate Education,
        1, Hume Street.